OVERCOMING
SEXUAL
IMMORALITY

BILL RUDGE

**LIVING TRUTH
PUBLISHERS**

Bill Rudge Ministries, Inc.
Hermitage, Pennsylvania
www.billrudge.org

Unless otherwise indicated, Scripture quotations are from the Holy Bible, New International Version, copyright © 1973, 1978, 1984 by the International Bible Society. Used by permission of Zondervan Publishing House. All rights reserved. References to the Deity have been capitalized.

Scripture quotations marked NAS are from the New American Standard Bible, copyright © 1960, 1962, 1963, 1968, 1971, 1972, 1973, 1975, 1977 by the Lockman Foundation. Used by permission.

Scripture quotations marked KJV are from the King James Version of the Bible.

Because of the sensitivity of this material, the names of people have been changed to protect them.

Overcoming Sexual Immorality
Copyright © 1992, 1996 by Bill Rudge
Updated and expanded edition copyright © 2008 by Bill Rudge
ISBN 978-1-889809-13-7

Published by Living Truth Publishers
A Division of Bill Rudge Ministries, Inc.
Hermitage, Pennsylvania
www.billrudge.org

Packaged by Pine Hill Graphics
Cover Design: Jay O. Gould

All rights reserved. No part of this publication may be reproduced, stored in a retrieval system or transmitted in any form by any means, electronic, mechanical, photocopy, recording, or otherwise, without prior permission of the author or publisher, except as provided by USA copyright law.

Printed in the United States of America

Contents

Introduction 4

Rampant Immorality 5

The Infiltrated Church 11

The Sexual Fantasy World Is Far from Reality 15

"But We're in Love" 21

The Bondage of Pornography 29

Not in My Home 40

The Media Connection 43

Even Heroes Suffer Consequences 51

God's Perspective 62

Steps to Overcoming Sexual Immorality 71

A Storybook Romance 90

A Modern-Day Love Story 100

Closing Comments 110

Introduction

The intent of this book is to motivate those who are pure to remain so and to help those who have been tainted to achieve victory by being restored to purity and peace. It was written from years of expreience for those who truly want to be set free and overcome sexual immorality.

It took me half a lifetime to learn the insights contained in this book, so you may have to read it several times to implement the principles contained within it.

As you read each chapter, may the Lord open your eyes to see the lies that have deceived so many. May He open your heart to receive something far surpassing and more fulfilling than any sexual experience. May you be so transformed that you will overcome and live victoriously, like the victor in a great contest. It will be worth every effort you put forth.

Rampant Immorality

Sandi was a beautiful young woman—athletic, intelligent, and involved in many college activities. It seemed as though everything was going her way. But the day I talked to her, she was broken and frightened. She fought back the tears as she tried to explain how she had gotten into this regrettable situation. Drifting from her relationship with God, *Sandi* had become promiscuous and self-indulgent, living each day for that day. Now she was pregnant, and to make matters worse, she was uncertain of the identity of the baby's father.

Jacob thought he had it all together until his wife fell in love with another man in their swingers' group. The nightmarish scenario that followed resulted in prison for him for an alleged double homicide of his wife and her lover, untold trauma on his children and family, and the untimely death of his mother.

Daniel was a good-looking, middle-aged married man with wandering eyes. His many sexual relationships with attractive young women marred his outspoken testimony for Christ. His wife suffered silently through years of his unfaithfulness.

Barb was a teen living with her mom and stepfather. Her stepfather sexually molested her. Unable to cope with being raped by her stepfather, she took an overdose of drugs, lapsed into a coma, and died a few days later.

Rob invited his recently divorced best friend to move in with him as he had no place to live. A few months later *Rob* came home early from work to discover his wife and best friend in bed. *Rob's* wife divorced him and married the other guy. *Rob* was forced to move out of his house while his former best friend moved in to live with *Rob's* ex-wife and children.

Kirk was a youth pastor. He was a seemingly positive influence in the lives of many young people—until he molested two boys. After being turned in to the local authorities, he fled the country. However, the boys were left to deal with the spiritual and emotional trauma.

David volunteered for a local youth organization. He appeared to be an excellent role model; however, *David* was shot to death by an angry father who accused him of molesting his son. It was soon discovered that he had molested many other children.

Beth was single and in her early twenties when she got involved with a married man. His wife found out and confronted her, so she terminated the relationship with her lover. He was not about to lose *Beth* so when she refused to continue the sexual relationship, he shot and killed her.

Bobby was a young teen who had consensual sex with a female classmate. A month later he was told that she was pregnant. The terror that overtook his life, like an unexpected strike of lightning, prompted him to strategize how to kill the baby or the mother if she refused to cooperate and have an abortion. He was consumed by fear for the future. A few months later, he was informed it was all a hoax, intended to punish him for dumping the girl after their brief sexual encounter.

Christy was at a party with a group of friends. Someone must have put something in her drink. She woke up the next morning in a back bedroom all alone, but knew she had been violated. Two months later she was diagnosed with a sexually transmitted disease.

Lenny was married and a popular pastor of a growing church. A sexual encounter with another woman led to serious marriage problems. Unwilling to accept counseling to save the marriage, he divorced his wife. He left a devastated family and congregation.

Jess and his wife were involved in ministry. He started drinking at a bar where he was supposedly witnessing to the patrons. His wife eventually, but reluctantly, started going with him to the bar. While he was busy flirting with other women, he did not realize that another guy was making a play for his wife. *Jess'* wife soon left him for the other man. With tears streaming down his face he told of the traumatic scenario that unfolded. He begged God to restore his marriage and pleaded with his wife to come back—but she never did.

Sonya began having sex as a young teen. She was taking birth control pills but still ended up pregnant a few years later. Her boyfriend wanted to marry her, but she refused. After having the baby, she broke up with him and soon became pregnant by another guy. *Sonya* and this guy live together in extreme poverty with two young children. She wants to leave the father of her second child because he treats her badly, but she has nowhere to go.

Paul was addicted to pornography. He concealed it from hiw wife for several years. When she did discover it, she divorced him. They both found out later that their teenage son years earlier had discovered his father's pornographic materials. As a young teen he was also addicted to pornography and had used his younger sister to experiment with some of the visuals he saw.

Danny and *Ann* were married and had two children. *Ann* met another man and ran away with him to another state. *Danny* did not see her or his children for several years. *Ann* eventually married the other man. A few years later *Ann* was devastated when her second husband left her for another woman.

Linda was happily married until she discovered she had herpes. She was confused because she had been a faithful wife. She soon discovered her husband contracted herpes while having an affair. Years of anger, guilt, and pain followed.

Shawn was a courageous Marine who conquered his enemies and fulfilled his commitment to the Marine Corps. Yet he could not fulfill his commitment to his wife or conquer his lustful passions. The Lord gave me a clear message for him, "Kill your lusts, or your lusts will kill you." The reality of those words soon surfaced as his continued sexual addiction ravaged his beautiful wife and children and anguished his life.

Mark was a vivid example of what someone can become if they do not repent of immorality. *Mark* looked like a living-dead person—ashen skin, unkempt hair, wild eyes, and slow speech and body movements. For over an hour *Mark* told his tale of misery, which he believes began at age 11 when he found his father's pornography. That led to over 30 years of unimaginable sexual addiction.

With quivering lips *Mark* said, "My sexual addiction has destroyed me." Thirty years of doctors, psychiatrists, medications, hospitalization, and untold grief to himself and his family left him a shell of a man. As tears streamed down *Mark's* face he asked the Lord to forgive him. He destroyed every vestige of pornography on his computer and in his home. It has been a long and difficult road, but with God's help, *Mark* is hoping to win this battle.

Andrew was only married a short time when he began having an affair. When his wife discovered it she left him, emotionally traumatized and forced to endure the struggles of being a single mother. Shortly thereafter on his way to visit his lover, *Andrew* was in a car accident. Confined to a wheelchair, he is attempting to get back with his ex-wife and their young child, but at this time that possibility is uncertain.

The High Price

These are only a few of innumerable examples I could share concerning adverse consequences of sexual promiscuity. The above scenarios have been played out countless times.

Maybe a tragic accident brings an unfaithful mate to their senses concerning the importance of a faithful marriage. Other times the unfaithful partner wakes up one day and realizes they really do love their former spouse—who is no longer interested in restoration or is remarried. Too many figure out too late they lost the best thing they ever had.

A sad irony is the price the unfaithful partner often pays in later years—and sometimes, as in *Andrew's* case, much sooner.

There are countless unfaithful partners who because of an accident, disease, or advancing age, are in desperate need of a caregiver. But the one who would have lovingly taken care of them is gone—prematurely dead or diseased—often by the very hand of the unfaithful partner who unleashed tremendous and destructive emotional stress on them earlier in their marriage.

Some unfaithful spouses who were able to salvage their marriages and stay together, later in life felt intense grief and remorse when they realized the health and youthfulness stolen from their partner was because of their unfaithfulness.

The high price of sexual immorality and unfaithfulness is sobering. Time and choices have a way of catching up as we eventually reap what we sow. One day the loss of what could have been and should have been is overwhelming and devastating. So make wise choices to minimize later regrets.

New Levels of Perversion

In spite of the threat of sexually transmitted diseases, pregnancy, ruined lives, broken families, and a host of other adverse consequences, sexual immorality is rampant today.

Pornography, prostitution, strip clubs, pre-marital sex, adultery, wife swapping, orgies, molestation, abuse, rape, exhibitionism, indecent exposure, sadomasochism, bestiality, necrophilia, pedophilia, and other erotica permeates our culture. In many aspects our decadent society takes the behavior of ancient pagan fertility rites to new levels of perversion.

This is a world given over to every sexual perversion imaginable. We are living in the midst of a culture in which people, driven by an insatiable appetite for erotica, unsuccessfully attempt to satisfy their unquenchable lusts for sexual gratification. The Bible says—

Having lost all sensitivity, they have given themselves over to sensuality so as to indulge in every kind of impurity, with a continual lust for more (Ephesians 4:19).

The Infiltrated Church

Though the sexual immorality in the world today is alarming, even more startling is how it has infiltrated so many churches. God's enemy is intent on getting Christians involved in pornography and illicit sexual relationships. His goal is to neutralize believers and render them powerless.

Satan relentlessly attempts to lure believers from pure devotion to Christ through the pursuit of pleasure and self-gratification. He knows that a compromised person is an ineffective tool for the Lord. While his main device is sexual enticements, he knows all our vulnerabilities and past weaknesses and will use any vice we have to seduce us.

Christian homes, churches, and ministries are being devastated by church members and leaders who are involved in pornography and adultery. Many are being tempted and seduced into a short season of pleasure. Then without warning they are thrust into some of the most oppressive and devastating consequences imaginable. Without God's intervention, it is impossible to escape this web of destruction the enemy weaves. One fallen man of God said to me, "You cannot imagine the evil and oppression Satan unleashed in my life and the joy and peace of the Lord he stole from me."

Is it any wonder Paul wrote in Colossians 3:5-8—

Put to death, therefore, whatever belongs to your earthly nature: sexual immorality, impurity, lust, evil desires and greed, which is idolatry. Because of these, the wrath of God is coming. You used to walk in these ways, in the life you once lived. But now you must rid yourselves of all such things....

A female inmate wrote an insightful letter to me, which gives a glimpse of the consequences of sexual immorality. Excerpts follow:

> I received your book *Overcoming Sexual Immorality*. Thank you for writing it. Most people do not realize how addictive sexual immorality really is. Also, once being in ministry myself it seems to be the very first sin the devil places on a platter of other pleasures for us to taste and enjoy.
>
> I turned my back on the Lord because of several things, but mostly because our pastor lived a double life. We found out he had been participating, along with a few other leaders, in orgies. He eventually ran off with a younger girl in the church. Before the pastor left, he made a pass at me, which hurt. After a year, I began to stray.
>
> Drinking and sex were the lures. I was burned out from working hard in ministry for eleven years, hurt, disillusioned and very confused. I realize these are not acceptable but they were very real to me then. I ran from God for ten years. In that time, alcoholism and sexual immorality were my life.
>
> My children were in their teens when I divorced my ministry partner, friend, and the father of my children. The first two years I drank constantly, had four nervous breakdowns, and many sexual partners. My sins continued until I came home as a prodigal

and my Heavenly Father was there waiting for me. Thank God for a second chance.

Because of my sin, I destroyed my family. I am serving a two to ten year sentence. I have served one year. Sexual immorality and drinking, with my full consent, destroyed my life. Now I am a Sex Offender.

The Lord has fully restored my two children and me. In this past year, the Lord has allowed me to sit in this regional jail waiting to be transported to prison. It has just been Jesus and me and all the Bible studies I can get. I am being remolded and polished to be of use to Him again. He has promised to fully restore my life and more. It took being charged and prison-bound to stop me.

Abstain from Sinful Desires

The apostle Peter says the following—

As obedient children, do not conform to the evil desires you had when you lived in ignorance. But just as He who called you is holy, so be holy in all you do. Dear friends, I urge you, as aliens and strangers in the world, to abstain from sinful desires, which war against your soul. For you have spent enough time in the past doing what pagans choose to do—living in debauchery, lust, drunkenness, orgies, carousing and detestable idolatry. They think it strange that you do not plunge with them into the same flood of dissipation, and they heap abuse on you. But they will have to give account to Him who is ready to judge the living and the dead (1 Peter 1:14,15; 2:11; 4:3-5).

Why I Gave It Up

Why did I give up the pleasures of my past that seemed so normal before I knew the Lord? There were three main reasons:

First, God's Word and Spirit revealed to me they are contrary to His plan and purpose for human beings.

Second, I became convinced they lead to destructive consequences—physically, mentally, emotionally, and spiritually.

Third, the Lord Jesus will one day establish His eternal kingdom, and I do not want to be excluded from it because of pursuing temporary sensual pleasures in willful disobedience and rebellion. Therefore, I am willing, by His grace, to give up anything now for the hope I have in Him.

Challenge to His People

During a recent time of prayer and fasting the Lord spoke to my heart to challenge His people to walk in holiness and purity. In spite of an increasingly corrupt and vile world, He is coming back for a Bride without spot or blemish. So it is time that His Church cleans up her act.

We will be tried and tested in our pursuit of holiness and purity. The enemy will use every opportunity and method to pollute our minds with vile images and compromise our lives in sinful behavior. We must resist by the power of His Spirit and Word.

This is a day and age for believers to evaluate our lives—examine what we are entertained by, contemplate what our minds are being exposed to, consider the words we speak, and ponder the meditations of our heart. It is a time to purify our lives and thoughts.

The Sexual Fantasy World Is Far from Reality

The first commandment of marketing gurus is the overused adage, "Sex sells!" Commercials, talk shows, reality TV programs, documentaries, and the news are laced with sexual language and imagery.

A restrictive moral climate is not tolerated as people demand uncensored freedom to do whatever they want. However, expression of every sexual passion imaginable only leads to slavish addiction. Titus 3:3 states—

At one time we too were foolish, disobedient, deceived and enslaved by all kinds of passions and pleasures....

Those who indulge in illicit sex or pornography set in motion a process that can quickly become uncontrollable. Destructive patterns develop which cause a person to struggle with immoral thoughts, lustful fantasies, and impulsive behavior. Guilt, worry, fear, stress, sickness, premature aging, sexually transmitted diseases, extramarital affairs, marriage problems, family chaos, and children following in their parents' footsteps, are often the price to be paid.

The sexual fantasy world created by the media is far from reality, but people try what they see. This encompasses every type of sexual activity conceivable—only to discover it is not as satisfying as the media's distorted and sensationalized portrayal led them to believe.

Two Worldviews

The lure of the world through television, movies, the Internet, music, magazines, and books can be hard to resist. However, if we do not resist, we will be infected with a philosophy and lifestyle which is diametrically opposed to God's revelation of truth and will ultimately destroy us.

First John 2:16,17 gives a clear perspective—

For everything in the world—the cravings of sinful man, the lust of his eyes and the boasting of what he has and does—comes not from the Father but from the world. The world and its desires pass away, but the man who does the will of God lives forever.

There are two opposing worldviews vying for our allegiance. One encourages us to flaunt our freedom by watching and indulging in whatever we desire. The other, which is God's perspective, calls us to maturity and purity. It tells us that fornication and adultery are contrary to His will and there should not even be a hint of sexual immorality among believers (Ephesians 5:3-5).

Since God is the Creator and knows what is ultimately best for His creation, wisdom dictates we submit to His perspective and avoid the adverse consequences of ignoring and disobeying His directives.

Those Who Triumphed

Besides numerous illustrations concerning the negative consequences I gave in chapter one, there are countless examples of those who triumphed by either avoiding involvement in sexual immorality or eventually being set free. The following are just a few—as well as others I will share throughout this book.

Chad's wife discovered he was viewing pornography on the Internet. Facing possible separation, he was motivated to get help. Christian counseling helped him to identify the root of his problem. Communication with and accountability to his wife and the Lord not only helped him to overcome his addiction, but also to help others who were struggling with addiction to pornography.

Wanda had a problem with alcohol and exhibitionism. She almost always dressed provocatively, but when she drank too much she let everything hang out. Her marriage was almost over because her husband did not know what to do with her. Some Christians befriended her and invited her and her husband to church. They both made a commitment to Christ and a marvelous transformation of their lives and marriage began.

Brad had an opportunity to begin an affair with an attractive woman. Realizing the adverse consequences he would inflict upon his life, he resisted the temptation. Fifteen years later he unexpectedly saw her. After seeing how unattractive she had become, he was appalled to think he almost lost his marriage and family for her, but grateful to the Lord for protecting him.

Bud and *Carol's* marriage was beyond hopeless. Before the final collapse, a friend recommended Marble Retreat, a Christian center for troubled marriages. The two weeks spent there helped to put their marriage back together better than it ever was before.

Angie had been promiscuous since she was a teen, following in the pattern of her mother. Now in her thirties and with a husband and children *Angie's* life was falling apart. Her sexual addiction and illicit relationships with numerous guys were destroying her life and marriage. Wanting the devastation to end, she asked the Lord's forgiveness. Realizing she truly wanted to be set free of her addiction, her husband stayed with her and together they committed their lives to the Lord and to the rebuilding of their marriage with His help.

Phil walked to the back of the commercial airline on which he was a passenger to use the facilities when a stewardess asked him if he was single. Thinking it concerned his seating assignment he inquired, "Why do you ask?" She pointed to an attractive stewardess as she told him her friend wanted to know. Having already made a covenant with the Lord not to get compromised in an illicit affair, he responded that he was married. As he walked back to his seat she said, "You have beautiful eyes." He thanked her and then headed back to his seat to rejoin his wife. During their drive home from the airport *Phil* mentioned to his wife about this encounter. His wife was pleased to have a faithful husband who resisted the advances of another woman.

Teri was a virgin and determined not only to remain one until marriage but also to marry a virgin. She met an attractive guy while in her teens who, although he had been offered sex by many beautiful girls, resisted the temptation because of his commitment to Christ. *Teri* and *John* dated for many years and although the temptations were intense, they stayed virgins until they married. Their testimonies and marital faithfulness are a great inspiration to many.

Samantha decided to quit the dating scene and not date again until she met the person she was going to marry. She learned from past experience to keep her list of requirements high—seemingly impossible. One day she met the man she was to marry. He had been forgiven by the Lord for past mistakes and fulfilled all the biblical and personal standards *Samantha* set. Their story of falling in love and life together is a powerful witness of God's forgiveness, faithfulness, and blessing.

Don, a middle-aged widower of eleven years, knows what a challenge it is to remain celibate and pure. He illustrates this by sharing the following scenario:

> Several months after the tragic death of her husband, I asked a co-worker out to dinner. *Dara's* kind and gentle disposition made her a good companion and we would frequently talk while at work. When

she asked if she could reciprocate the dinner one afternoon while she was on call, I accepted.

After dinner, she would have had to return to the medical facility where we worked and wait in the drab "on call" room. I thought it would be a nice gesture to show her my home and let her spend that time there instead. As we sat on the couch together talking, she suddenly made a suggestion we go upstairs to my bedroom and have some fun.

In amazement I was able to tell her in a cracking voice, "I don't think so!" Ten minutes after this proposition, my seventeen-year-old son and a friend unexpectedly came through the front door. I was horrified to think of the impression he would have had if I had said yes to *Dara's* proposition. My son would have been stunned and disappointed if he had seen us fumbling half clothed to shut the bedroom door. The story would no doubt spread to his siblings. My efforts to raise all my children properly on the issue of purity would be negated. I would have to repent and try to recover the credibility that would surely have been lost.

Dara called me the next day to apologize for her behavior. I wonder if during her trip to the bathroom she had noticed the Bill Rudge ministry newsletter on sexual purity that was stacked on top of my other reading material.

I am grateful to God this episode ended as it did, in obedience, rather than giving in to a willing partner who offered me a momentary pleasurable experience, which would have resulted in dire consequences.

So Many More Stories to Tell

There are many more illustrations I could share about God's forgiveness and restoration or of adults and teens who have remained untainted from the stains of immorality and triumphed in the midst of strong temptation.

Over the years I have met many single people who have remained virgins and also married couples whose faithful relationship to each other and the Lord has resulted in untold blessing, peace, and joy. Instead of settling for quick gratification, they clothed themselves in wisdom, strength, and self-control.

Their stories would take volumes to tell because, like a beautiful chrysalis, the multitudes of blessings attained take a lifetime to unfold. However, the principles they live by will be revealed throughout the pages of this book.

"But We're in Love"

Many youth "hook-up" for a casual sexual encounter. They think there are no strings attached, but invisible cords—like unseen parasites in the bloodstream—begin to envelop their thoughts, attitudes, and behavior.

Then there are those young people who reason, "We love each other, so what harm is there in having a physical relationship?" Yet, this only reveals that the true meaning of the word love has been lost in our culture. According to the Bible, if you love someone, you want the best for that person, and you are patient with them. First Corinthians 13:4-7 says—

> *Love is patient, love is kind...it is not self-seeking, it is not easily angered...does not delight in evil but rejoices with the truth. It always protects....*

Shawn, whose story you read a brief overview of in chapter one, related the following concerning his and *Edith's* early dating experience—

> *Edith* was a believer in Christ, I was not. I thought premarital sex would cement our relationship but it did the opposite. My coercing her into premarital sex caused guilt and resentment in her towards me, which was the beginning of our emotional separation.

Being pressured to prove you love your boyfriend or girlfriend by giving them what they want or being coerced to satisfy their sexual desires is not love, but lust.

If your *lover* really cared about you and really desired the best for you, he or she would want to protect you from anyone—including himself or herself—who might hurt you. Asking you to do something that violates your convictions, risks immediate or long-term adverse consequences, and jeopardizes your future happiness is not love—it is selfishness and foolishness.

One day your boyfriend uses promises of undying love in a passionate attempt to seduce you, but what happens once he is satisfied? What happens if a car wreck disfigures your face? What happens if a degenerative disease ravages your body? Will he reject you? True love is much deeper than physical attraction and should be based on a strong and lasting commitment.

The one who truly loves you will be there if you lose a leg in a tragic accident or are maimed on the field of battle. A faithful partner will stay with you even though disease or age decreases your beauty.

The Sexual Revolution

I was a teen during the 1960's sexual revolution. Before it started, most guys and girls were virgins. An honorable girl required a marriage license before she would have sex. A guy wanting intimacy with his girlfriend had to patiently wait until she married him.

My generation changed all that. My friends and I did everything possible and used every line imaginable to weaken girls' resistance. We took advantage of the growing sexual revolution to exploit our self-centered sexual desires. Our slogan was, "Free love and free sex." We would brag and laugh about our conquests, often sharing tangible evidence.

The following comments concerning Woodstock and the apostle Paul's perspective on casual sex are excerpted from

None of These Diseases, a fascinating book by S.I. McMillen, M.D. and David E. Stern, M.D.—

During three days in August 1969 on a farm near Woodstock, New York, the youth of America declared the founding of the "Woodstock Nation"—the land of sex, drugs, and rock 'n' roll. A huge crowd of 500,000 camped in a muddy meadow. There they wallowed in free sex, illegal drugs, and angry music.

They got what they wanted. But did they want what they got? They wanted free sex. For a lifetime they got herpes, genital warts, PID, and a host of other STDs.

The Apostle Paul grew up in the pagan city of Tarsus, where a visitor complained that you couldn't walk in the streets without hearing the panting and grunting of brothel customers. Since Paul grew up surrounded by this cesspool of bawdy sex, you might expect his writings to embrace casual sex; but Paul's writings made a clean break from Roman culture. In effect, Paul urged believers, when in Rome, do not do as the Romans: "God wants you to live differently from those around you and to avoid loose sex. Treat your own bodies with dignity and respect. Don't abuse them in lustful passion, as your godless neighbors do" (1 Thess. 4:3-5).

A Proper Time...A Proper Place

Many justify sexual sin with the excuse, "Sex is natural, so why fight it?" But so is fire! Controlled, it provides light and warmth. Uncontrolled, it ravages and destroys. Just ask the people I met while serving as a chaplain during the California wildfires.

The excitement of illicit sex is short-lived. More often than not, it leads to fears and tears. Fear of an unwanted pregnancy or of contracting an incurable disease or of being caught, and tears from broken relationships and the shattered trust of one's partner.

The best protection against sexually transmitted diseases is to practice mutual faithfulness with one lifetime spouse. Isn't it interesting this is exactly what God commanded from the beginning?

Within the framework of a God-ordained marital relationship, sex is one of the most pleasurable experiences this side of Heaven. After all, He invented it with all its passion and excitement. The Song of Solomon in the Bible introduces us to the wonder and passion of sexuality.

God designed marital sex for pleasure and procreation. The feelings and emotions generated in a trusting and faithful marriage make the sexual experience far more intense and enjoyable. But sex outside of marriage can be very destructive.

Sex is powerful enough to create a new life. Then you have several choices. You can have an abortion. Yet God gives no one the right to take an innocent life. Besides, the long-term consequences of an abortion are staggering. You can give the baby up for adoption or attempt to raise the child yourself. However, these choices are very difficult and will result in a scenario that radically affects many lives. You can get married, but such marriages are usually turbulent and rarely last.

It is much wiser to follow God's advice and wait to have sex until you are in a loving and committed marriage.

A good motto for youth and unmarried adults is: "Hands off. Clothes on." Avoid being alone with your boyfriend or girlfriend, and instead of sexual discussions, talk more about your faith and biblical convictions.

Ran Away and Married

As new Christians in our teens, my girlfriend and I desired to live for the Lord and not sin against Him, so we ran away and got married. Although we had not yet read the following verse, we unknowingly did what it said—

But if they cannot control themselves, they should marry, for it is better to marry than to burn with passion (1 Corinthians 7:9).

I was also blessed to marry a virgin—something I did not deserve, but for which I was greatly appreciative. Although our marriage was given little hope by anyone, and almost ended early on, with the Lord's help, we are one of the few teen marriages to survive and flourish.

Self-Control: A Mark of True Love
According to BJ Rudge, Ph.D.—

Self-control is a highly esteemed virtue in the Bible but is no longer an esteemed quality in today's culture, especially in regard to sexuality. The motto of our culture is simply to live in the present and enjoy the moment as we allow our passions to control us. "If it feels right, then just do it" has become the defining mark in the expression of "true love" between a man and a woman.

The main tragedy that has resulted from this type of thinking has not only been a proliferation of STDs, unwanted pregnancies, and extramarital affairs leading to divorce, but a culture of people who have never experienced the beauty of truly loving someone or being truly loved by another.

In contrast to self-fulfilled lust that seeks self-gratification, the Bible calls us to live a life of self-control (1 Peter 1:13; 4:7; 5:8). The Word of God commands Christians to resist "…ungodliness and worldly passions, and to live self-controlled, upright and godly lives in this present age" (Titus 2:12).

A healthy and godly relationship is not built upon self-pleasing lust, but upon self-controlled love. In fact, self-control is a mark of true love because it reminds us not to look at another person merely as a means to fulfill our lusts and desires, but to seek in them a worthy and virtuous end.

Are You Being Conditioned?

A young man told me he could not keep his hands off his girlfriend. He justified his behavior by reasoning that at least they were not "going all the way." Besides, they planned to get married some day. I explained premarital sex—even with one's future spouse—makes both more vulnerable to extra-marital affairs.

When I explained he was weakening her resistance to be victimized by someone else later on, he quickly realized he did not want her being vulnerable to other guys now, or in the future if he married her.

What will happen during an extended illness or being away on a business trip? When boredom occurs or temptation arises, those who were conditioned to receive instant gratification are more likely to have an extra-marital encounter in the future.

In contrast, I told this young man if he and his girlfriend showed self-control when they were together, they would be more inclined to show self-restraint when they were apart—reducing the risk of being enticed or seduced by someone else after marriage.

That is why when I meet with couples who want to get married; I encourage them to refrain from sexual activity from that point on. I point out that of all the girls and guys in the world, they have chosen each other. By exercising self-discipline over sexual desires with each other now, it will affair-proof their marriage later.

Keeping Yourself Pure

Regarding sex, God says, "Wait till marriage and keep it only between you and your spouse." There is a time and a place for everything, and in this case, after the wedding is the time and your marriage partner is the place.

It was not easy in the apostle Paul's day and it is not easy today to keep one's heart and mind pure. Merely a turn of the head or an innocent glance of the eyes can reveal sights and provoke thoughts, that if left unrestrained, would lead to anything but purity.

Nevertheless, everyone who has the hope of one day seeing and being with Christ "purifies himself, just as He is pure" (1 John 3:3).

Like a young virgin saving herself for her husband on their wedding night, we must strive to be spiritually and morally pure. Keeping our thoughts and lives unpolluted is a command, a challenge, and a believer's calling.

Learn the Lesson of the Oak Tree

While driving to the airport and pondering my message for an upcoming speaking engagement, I noticed a large fallen oak tree split down the middle by an apparent lightning strike. After I glanced at that massive tree I contemplated how it took a lifetime for it to reach its full potential and stately beauty, but fell to the ground in a brief moment by a random bolt of lightning. So, too, a lifetime of virtue can be forever tarnished in one random passionate moment.

Both nature and hormones, although intended by our Creator to be a purposeful blessing, can become a destructive curse if they get out of control. While a tree cannot protect itself from the forces of nature, you can and must safeguard yourself from the devastating forces of sexual immorality.

I Knew a Couple

I knew a couple who had a great marriage. In comparison to almost everyone else, their marriage was very good, but it could have been even better. While dating, and during the beginning of their marriage, they were careless. In spite of forgiveness and deep love, neither one totally trusted the other. She wanted his love and attention, and although he gave much to her, try as hard as he might, he could not give his total self to her. She sensed this and as a result they both suffered.

They loved each other deeply, but something was missing because they each had given a part of themselves away. Although neither of them could live without the other, it was sometimes hard for them to live together. Most of their problems stemmed back to when they had violated each other's trust.

One day they realized they had not truly forgiven each other. He also realized he did not love her as Christ loved the church so he repented and attempted to do so, which greatly improved their relationship. A life-threatening disease forced them to forget the past and focus even more on loving each other. She needed his total love and commitment and he gave it to her as best as he could. The restoration of her trust in him, and the security she felt because of his faithfulness, proved crucial in her return to health.

If only they had obeyed God's guidelines from their youth, they could have avoided all the scarring and trauma they put each other through for so many years. By God's grace they are now experiencing the kind of marriage God intended from the beginning.

They have discovered that a lifetime is not long enough to be with the one you love.

The Bondage of Pornography

With just the click of a remote control or computer mouse, a person can instantly enter a fantasy world of sexual promiscuity. As television programs and movies become more explicit and Internet access becomes unlimited, the seductive domain of pornography, where all sorts of erotica and perversions are manifested, is available to virtually anyone at any time.

Countless people are entangled in a web of immorality because the lure of the flesh and the world is so strong. Many Christians have compromised biblical truth and personal convictions to become slaves once again to the corruption and darkness from which Christ delivered them. As a result, those losing their peace, health, and marriage are mounting.

Before you get caught (or continue, if you are already entrapped) in this downward slide into compromise and bondage, consider the following:

1) Intruder Alert

Pornography is an intruder in your home and life. Just as you would fight and resist an invader seeking to molest, rape, or kill your family, so too, you must fight and resist this intruder because it will destroy your family. It also wastes your time, drains your energy, and ages you prematurely.

2) Violates Trust

Every girl and guy is someone's daughter or son. Certainly no reasonable parent raises their child to be a sex object. Nor do they give them in marriage to be exploited or cheated on by their mate.

Therefore, pornographic indulgences and illicit sexual encounters violate the trust of those who give their daughters and sons in marriage. It violates your wedding vows. It violates your commitment to the Lord. And it violates yourself—as it is a sin against your own body (1 Corinthians 6:18).

3) It Is Degrading

Temptation often strikes when you are bored or alone. People enact deeds in darkness, which they would be ashamed of in public.

Everyone involved in pornography is degraded. Those who pose nude often regret it later. Those caught viewing pornography by their spouse or children are usually humiliated and experience a loss of respect, which is difficult to regain.

Scripture indicates what is done in secret will eventually be openly exposed. If not in this life, then in the one to come. You will stand before your Creator and give an account of every secret thought and hidden sin.

4) Adultery

The Bible strongly condemns adultery. Jesus clarified the meaning of adultery to include lusting in one's heart. Therefore, viewing pornography, mentally undressing someone, visualizing a sexual encounter, or fantasizing life and romance with another, are in reality adultery (Matthew 5:28).

Memories of pornographic visuals and sexual experiences can remain in the mind's eye for a lifetime—manifesting unexpectedly or at will—causing mental or verbal comparisons, criticisms, and conflicts. Lingering pornographic images can incite recurring lustful thoughts, temptations, and adultery in one's heart.

5) Will Not Inherit the Kingdom of God

Scripture is clear that those who live a life of wanton sexual promiscuity will not inherit the kingdom of God. A few examples follow:

1 Corinthians 6:9,10—

...Do not be deceived: Neither the sexually immoral nor idolaters nor adulterers...will inherit the kingdom of God.

Galatians 5:19-21—

The acts of the sinful nature are obvious: sexual immorality, impurity and debauchery...orgies, and the like. I warn you, as I did before, that those who live like this will not inherit the kingdom of God.

Revelation 21:8—

But the cowardly, the unbelieving, the vile, the murderers, the sexually immoral...their place will be in the fiery lake of burning sulfur. This is the second death.

Revelation 22:15—

Outside [God's Holy City] are the dogs, those who practice magic arts, the sexually immoral....

In New Testament times the term "dogs," when applied to people, referred to anyone of low moral character. Such people will not be permitted to enter God's eternal kingdom.

When Scripture condemns the sexually immoral, it is not referring to those who may be struggling to overcome sexual sin. It is in reference to those who say, "This is the way I am. I am going to keep living this lifestyle. It is your problem, God, not mine."

6) It Grieves His Spirit

The Holy Spirit is grieved every time a believer indulges in pornography and looks upon naked or scantily clad bodies. Instead of being conformed to the likeness of Christ and glorifying God with our bodies and minds—He is dishonored. The fallout is far reaching because nothing is worse than losing a sense of His presence in our lives.

However, repentance and restoration are only a prayer away. Nothing is more satisfying than being in right relationship with the Lord. Mental purity is far more conducive to peace and internal youthfulness than a corrupt and polluted mind.

7) Spiritual Stronghold

Pornography offers immediate gratification, but the spirit of lust is never satisfied. While the excitement of the moment seems irresistible, when you give in to the lure of pornography, you allow the enemy access to your mind and heart, creating a spiritual stronghold for him.

Lusting after naked flesh intensifies and ultimately descends into more degenerate visuals and activities that lead to deeper bondage, emptiness, and despair.

Do not deceive yourself into thinking this will be your last look. There is always something new and a little more tantalizing that will lure you—unless you determine that your last look is already past.

There is nothing of value in pornographic web sites, magazines, or strip clubs—only despair, disease, death, and destruction. Opening your life to these images and behavior can be a quick road to bondage that can result in intense internal and spiritual warfare. It is not surprising many spiritual, emotional, and marital problems can be traced to pornography.

As you resist the temptations and repeatedly walk—or run—away from them, this stronghold will eventually diminish. Each victory makes you stronger and weakens the enemy's hold on your life.

8) Prepare to Suffer

When you are enticed to look at pornographic web sites, view sensual movies, watch exotic dancers, leaf through pornographic magazines, or have an illicit sexual encounter, prepare to suffer. The few minutes of satisfaction will be short-lived, followed by a sense of guilt, shame, disgust, and misery until you are brought to repentance.

The psalmist learned from experience—

Before I was afflicted I went astray, but now I obey Your word. It was good for me to be afflicted so that I might learn Your decrees (Psalm 119:67,71).

The apostle Peter tells us—

He who has suffered in his body is done with sin. As a result, he does not live the rest of his earthly life for evil human desires, but rather for the will of God (1 Peter 4:1,2).

When you are in the midst of extreme pain or feel like you are close to death you do not want your life filled with images or attitudes that dishonor the Lord.

9) Reap What Is Sown

If you cheat on your spouse—even through pornography—be assured that while you are indulging in your fantasy, the enemy is seeking someone or something to lure away your spouse and family members. He is working behind the scenes to destroy more than just you. He knows when you are compromised and neutralized, he can have easy access to your loved ones.

King David's sexual sins ultimately resulted in the unleashing of perverse immorality in his family—victimizing not only him, but those he dearly loved.

Fear, guilt, confusion, loss of health, and other negative consequences are the end product reaped from the sowing of sexual sin. Too many have weakened their marriages, lost their spouse and family through divorce, hurt or devastated their children, tarnished their testimony, and grew old before their time.

10) Show It All

Pornographic magazines and web sites want the freedom to "show it all." Then let them show it all—by including pictures of genital herpes, gonorrhea, syphilis, AIDS, and other STDs. And while they are at it, why not show the aborted babies, broken marriages, devastated children, and ruined lives?

I had not seen pornography for many years until a hacker sabotaged two of our ministry videos posted on another Christian web site. While doing the monthly monitoring of our videos, vile and disgusting pornographic images manifested on the computer screen. We immediately removed our videos from that site so no unsuspecting person would be enticed and entrapped.

It was interesting how my perspective on pornography had so drastically changed. What before knowing Christ was attractive and pleasurable, had become pathetic and repulsive. It actually sickened me for several days as the images slowly faded from my mind's eye. I felt sorry for the people displayed in the visuals because they are the real victims—used to make someone money, probably riddled with disease, or soon to be, and empty, unfulfilled.

My perspective has so changed that purity and righteousness—which are getting harder to find because of the aggressive tactics of the pornographers—are far more attractive than sensuality and immorality. We need to keep this concept in mind because what we think we want now, may later in life, repulse and sicken us.

Wandering Eyes

No believer or Christian leader should have wandering eyes or stare lustfully. It is degrading to yourself, your spouse, and your Lord. God will eventually bring judgment on those "flirting with their eyes" (Isaiah 3:16-24).

We must be more concerned about the condition of someone's heart than the shape of their body. We must be more concerned about their eternal destiny than desirous of a fleeting glimpse of their anatomy.

The most beautiful people in the world will in a few short years become unattractive. They will lose their *perfect* body and good looks as they begin to sag and wrinkle. Just go into a nursing home and compare the residents to their youthful pictures. Life goes by too quickly to sell out the Lord for a few years of fleeting pleasure.

Psalm 103:15-18 accurately states—

As for man, his days are like grass, he flourishes like a flower of the field; the wind blows over it and it is gone, and its place remembers it no more. But from everlasting to everlasting the Lord's love is with those who fear Him, and His righteousness with their children's children—with those who keep His covenant and remember to obey His precepts.

My prayer is that when someone looks into my eyes, they do not see lust, but the love and peace of Jesus Christ.

Dress Modestly with Decency

An informative footnote on 1 Timothy 2:9, in *The Full Life Study Bible,* indicates that it is God's will for Christians to dress modestly and discreetly. Excerpts follow—

The word "decency" (Greek *aidos*) implies a certain shame in exposing the body. It involves a refusal to dress in such a way as to draw attention to the body and to pass the boundaries of proper reserve. The source of modesty is in a person's heart or inner character. In other words, modesty is the outward manifestation of an inward purity.

Dressing immodestly, which may excite impure desires in others, is as wrong as the immoral desire it provokes. No activity or condition justifies the wearing of immodest attire that would expose the body in such a way as to stimulate lust in someone else (Galatians 5:13; Titus 2:11,12).

It is a sad commentary on any church when the biblical standard for modest dress is ignored and the world's customs are passively adopted. In a day of sexual permissiveness, the church should act and dress differently from a corrupt society that throws aside and ridicules the Spirit's desire for modesty, purity and godly restraint (Romans 12:1,2).

Romance Novels

Women's romance novels, love stories, and "chick flicks" can be equally as dangerous as men's pornographic magazines. Dr. Harry W. Schaumburg points this out in his book *False Intimacy: Understanding the Struggle of Sexual Addiction*—

> While most men are sexually stimulated by visual cues, reading romance novels and fantasizing may be the female counterpart. Romance novels are more than entertainment; they are sexually stimulating. Women can not only read them; they can "borrow" the romance. Such false intimacy with no risk is essentially no different from the intent of a man who hires an escort service. Most Christian women rightfully

object to men having explicit sexual material such as *Playboy*, but some of those same women would be offended if anyone suggested romance novels be banned. Seductive images come in both pictures and words, but both provide a false intimacy.

The Road to Adultery

Purity involves more than just avoiding blatant sexually stimulating images and situations. We must guard our hearts against even seemingly innocent flirtations and encounters and be more concerned about the Lord's opinion than impressing our friends with stories of sexual prowess.

The road to adultery often has many preliminary stages. Recognizing them early on and circumventing them can avert the slippery slope that leads to adultery. Something as seemingly innocent as a glance or wink of the eye can be all it takes to send a message of receptivity. An article in the *Alliance of Biblical Pentecostals*' newsletter stated—

> For a believer to commit adultery, many other sins must first be committed without repentance. For instance, the initial lust in the heart for another that is not their spouse; the "innocent" conversations with the other person who initiated an impure relationship; the casual or "accidental" touches; the secret rendezvous for a cup of coffee. All these things are sins and the Holy Spirit would most assuredly convict the believer of such things immediately. But if the voice of the Spirit goes unheeded, the believer can progress further and further down a road of sin until the final, horrible act of adultery takes place.

A Word to Victims

Victims of adultery and molestation often experience a lifetime of suffering and trauma in exchange for the brief perverted pleasure achieved by the adulterer or molester. Emotions generated within the victims churn like the relentless waves of the sea before a great storm. Revenge often becomes a controlling force in their lives.

Many victims of marital infidelity fall into the trap of retaliating against a spouse who is involved in an affair or other form of sexual immorality by doing likewise. They justify their illicit relationships or pornographic indulgences by blaming their unfaithful partner. An immoral lifestyle is a futile attempt to make one's unfaithful partner pay for their offenses.

Believers must never forget their own sexual purity is not contingent upon that of their spouse, but ultimately because of the Lord. He is our motivation to remain morally pure.

Even beauties are cheated on by their partners. But as a relationship expert accurately stated, "Partners cheat due to their own problems—anger, boredom, jealousy, sexual addiction—not due to something lacking in the women [or men]."

Both victim and victimizer must learn a valuable lesson from Scripture. Even though David realized that he had tragically wronged several people, he knew his ultimate wrong was against God—to whom he must ultimately answer. That is why he said during his prayer of repentance recorded in Psalm 51:4, "Against You, You only, have I sinned and done what is evil in Your sight." Sexual immorality is ultimately between each person and the Lord.

Adulterers and molesters are indeed pathetic and pitiful people who will eventually pay for their offenses. But all of us are desperate sinners in need of the Savior's mercy and forgiveness. We cannot expect the Lord to forgive us our greater wrongs against Him if we do not forgive those who have hurt us (Matthew 6:14,15; Colossians 3:13).

Any victims who are believers in Christ must not allow bitterness or personal revenge to consume their lives. Instead, they must release their pain and emotions to the Lord and trust Him to bring good out of every circumstance they face (Romans 8:28).

Instead of turning to alcohol, drugs, or other vices, the victim must take back control of his or her life with the Lord's help. Exercising, eating healthy, and becoming active in beneficial and fulfilling pursuits such as helping others, is great therapy. The apostle Paul's advice to forget those things behind us and to press on toward the goal of our calling in Christ Jesus is crucial.

A couple who discovered each other's unfaithfulness chose the path of forgiveness, but resolved never to tolerate such behavior in either of them again. A blessed marriage resulted as the previously unfaithful spouses were motivated to never stray again.

Victims of sexual abuse or unfaithfulness who identify with the suffering of Jesus Christ will find comfort and hope. Scripture indicates in this life believers will face trials and tragedies. The experiences of our hurts and pain help us to "participate in the sufferings of Christ" (1 Peter 4:12-16). Our personal suffering in this life gives us a glimpse of Christ's incomprehensible suffering for the sins of the world and helps us to appreciate His sacrificial love and marvelous grace.

I have repeatedly observed that the victims of unfaithfulness often have their pain and humiliation replaced with mercy and pity. Later in life, they often become the caregiver for the unfaithful partner whose life's choices led to the adverse consequences God warned about.

Most encouraging is the fact believers have the assurance that one day the memory of all past failures, hurts, and humiliations will be forever removed. The blessings and glory we ultimately receive will far surpass anything we might suffer or endure in this life (Romans 8:18).

Not in My Home

The following article was written by Cliff McNeely and is sure to be an eye-opening challenge.

You may think me crazy, but lately, several nights a week, I've invited strange, and sometimes obscene, people into my home—people I don't really know and with whom I would normally not associate. They show up at around 7 p.m. most evenings and leave right at 10 p.m. I can ask them to leave at anytime but I don't. I just sit there, usually not saying a word, and let them do pretty much whatever they want until they decide it's time to leave.

The other night, one of my new acquaintances, Donna, ordered her husband, Jimmy, to make love to her right then and there in my living room. She said that if he didn't, she'd know her pregnant body repulsed him. A couple of weeks ago, a guy named Calvin and a woman (I don't recall her name) showed up in my house. They evidently were going to be rooming together in an apartment. And while he thought she was a lesbian, she thought he was gay. It turns out they were both heterosexuals; but before they realized their misjudgment, they had a fairly explicit sexual conversation while I listened in.

And speaking of homosexuals, I recall another evening in the more recent past when a married man named Ford announced to his wife, right there in my home, that he was gay. And then I listened in as another man phoned Ford and asked him out on a date. This really made me uncomfortable but, again, I did or said nothing to discourage this from happening in my own home.

About a week before the above incident, and I'm terribly ashamed to tell this story, a man named Peter brought a prostitute into my home. I watched as he solicited sex from her and then, to my horror, she began to undress right there in front of me. They had a sexual conversation so repugnant that I can't even repeat its content. I heard words that night I would never use in my own home. And all the while I sat there unmoved, passively taking it all in.

While sitting in church last week, an image came to mind of a woman standing in my living room. In the image, this woman's husband, his mistress, and several of their friends were also there with us in the room. And this woman, in an attempt to humiliate her husband, unbuttoned her shirt and bared her breasts to everyone. Again, the image was somewhat fuzzy but nonetheless disturbing. But when these kinds of things occur with so much regularity in my home, it's virtually impossible for me to stop the memories from resurfacing at random in my mind.

I've even sat by without response as people I don't even know have had the gall to ridicule my faith and my God right in front of me, in my own home! They've mocked and stereotyped Christians as fanatical, hypocritical and insulting. I've also witnessed unspeakable acts of violence, rape, and torture. I fear I will never be rid of these negative and damaging memories. I wish now I would have said something, done something, to keep these obscene things from happening under my roof, in the sanctuary of my own home.

The sad fact is that these same obscene and violent acts are happening in millions of homes all across America... every time a TV set is turned on without forethought and discernment. That's right, every one of the scenes and conversations described above have happened on network television over the past few weeks.

Only you can control who or what comes into your home. Before sitting down in front of the set tonight for an evening of seemingly harmless entertainment, ask yourself the following questions: Who have I invited into my living room lately through my TV set? Would I allow the same kinds of conversations and actions to happen in my home in real life? How is watching these kinds of shows benefiting or harming myself and my family? And finally, if Jesus Christ were sitting beside me, what would I watch on TV, if anything?

(*Preview Family Movie & TV Review*, October 12, 1999. Used by permission.)

The Media Connection

Sexual immorality was rampant in the ancient Roman Empire. Banquets often degenerated into orgies. Many cities the apostle Paul ministered in were noted for temple prostitutes, brothels, and promiscuity. In the Roman culture of his day, this type of behavior was acceptable, but Paul revealed to the Gentile converts that sexual immorality was not acceptable to God.

Paul's words to the early church are as relevant today as they were then. He reminds us God calls believers to a higher standard and requires us to "live self-controlled, upright and godly lives" (Titus 2:12).

That Is Disgusting

Several years ago as I was heading home through a nearby neighborhood, I witnessed a disgusting behavior. I thought, "That is repulsive. How could anyone do such a thing?"

Have you ever seen someone do something disgusting? While it may have been repulsive to you, it was obviously acceptable to the person or persons doing it.

Consider for a moment *your* behavior and activities. Are any of them disgusting or detestable to God? If we believe God created us and Scripture is His revelation of truth, then it is imperative we learn what is pleasing to Him so we can do it and what is displeasing to Him and avoid it.

Proverbs 8:13 tells us that to fear the Lord is to hate evil. Evil and sin are anything that is contrary to His nature or will. Ephesians 5:10 admonishes us to find out what pleases the Lord.

What Are Your Standards?

I have discovered people like to condemn those who have lower standards than themselves and to mock those who have higher ones. It is also interesting to note people with lesser convictions like to pressure those with higher convictions to compromise them. Yet they rarely want to elevate their own. Nevertheless, everyone—even those who deny it—have a code of conduct by which they live.

When a Christian comments that my convictions regarding television are too strict, I ask them, "Do you watch pornography in your home?" Most quickly respond, "No!" I then point out that there are those who think their standard of not watching pornography is restrictive and self-righteous. They usually get the message.

The real question is, "Will your standards and mine really matter if they are not God's?" Will He say, "At least you did not do this, therefore you did well." It may be commendable that you do not tolerate blatant nudity and sex acts in your home, but do you allow swearing, profanity, crude and vulgar comments, or sexual humor and innuendos?

Are you a biblical or a cultural Christian? Do you live by the truth and principles in God's Word or merely conform to the world? Does your life reflect the values and philosophies of a corrupt generation and compromised church?

God's standard is filling our lives and homes with that which reflects His nature, brings glory to Him, and is truly beneficial to our well-being.

Something Is Wrong

The sad reality is many undiscerning Christians are addicted to television. They justify their tolerance of obscene language and sexually suggestive content by explaining they see and hear more than that at work or school. While we are not responsible for what we have no control over, we are accountable for what we do have control over; entertainment definitely falls into that category.

Persecution of Christians increases worldwide. The return of Christ draws nearer as the Lord desires faithful followers to share the Gospel with a lost and dying world. Yet, something is wrong when professing Christians and pastors watch without any conviction or remorse programs laced with profanity and immorality.

As you see the Day of the Lord approaching, or realize how much closer you are to eternity, your priorities had better change.

Conviction Leads to a No Television Fast

Although my family had limited television time and maintained strong guidelines, during a time of prayer and fasting I began to feel deep conviction. So in July of 1998, my wife and I made a fast unto the Lord we would not watch television in our home. We determined our home and ministry center would be an oasis in the midst of an increasingly corrupt world.

Only family videos and profitable programs of research or news of significant importance would be welcome. It is amazing how much more time we have for Bible study, prayer, and ministry. Even my children commented on how much calmer the atmosphere had become.

Why Do I Keep TV Out of My Home?

Why have I kept secular television out of my home for all these years? Because a few programs a week would undermine my family's commitment to Christ? No. But I do believe television has destroyed the spiritual lives of more believers and pastors than probably anything else. If we are to win the battle of overcoming sexual immorality, we must achieve victory over television.

I also believe the media's influence is becoming so strong that those who spend time watching secular television have little possibility to hear God's voice and to know His will. Besides, I do not want to sit in my home being entertained by something that often mocks my Lord and is ruining the spiritual life of many believers. I do not want my example to cause anyone to stumble.

The powerful influence of the media was vividly manifest several years ago when I returned to a small Caribbean island to minister. Ten years earlier the adults and youth were simple village people untainted by the media, but when I returned, the whole generation of youth was different—body piercings, tatoos, skimpy clothes, and hanging out at the mall. I asked one of the pastors sponsoring me if I had missed this part of their culture when I was there ten years earlier. He assured me it was not there then, but informed me this generation recently became like this from the influence of cable television, movies, music, and the Internet.

I used to think the Amish were hypocritical for disallowing telephones in their homes and not owning vehicles, yet they will use someone else's phone or accept a ride in someone else's vehicle. However, after hearing their explanation that they are merely trying to limit worldly influences in their lives by keeping modern conveniences out of their homes, I somewhat understand the reasoning for their lifestyle—even though I do not necessarily agree with their definition of worldliness.

Because of the wickedness of the house of Eli, God removed the priesthood from his family. I did not want the influence of television to negate the call of God on my life or family.

My desire is to have a house and ministry center filled with the presence of the Lord—free from the seductive influence of immorality oozing from many of the movies, talk shows, documentaries, and commercials into the minds and hearts of family members and guests.

Many Are Desensitized

As I made my home an oasis, I noticed my emotions and desires changing even more. I began to look at sexual immorality through new eyes. I saw it from God's perspective and realized how twisted and perverted His intended purpose for sex had become.

After not seeing television programs or commercials for many months, and then being exposed to them at airports or in other people's homes, it became obvious how many Christians are desensitized by the media and do not discern the rapid degeneration of our society. Like the proverbial frog in the pot of water on the stove, the heat is being turned up and few recognize the extreme dangers and consequences.

It is amazing that what was sleazy, hard core porn movies covertly shown when I was a youth are now overtly viewed by young people at movie theaters and in their homes on videos or computers. Even decent movies have previews of upcoming movies that often taint the minds of children.

How can our youth be exposed to so much seduction, nudity, and sex acts and not be influenced to experiment? Truly we are in a battle for the minds and souls of our young people—and us adults as well—as the pornification of our society accelerates.

What About Guests?

You may wonder what to do when you have guests in your home or you are a guest at someone else's home? I know it is awkward to turn off the television or change the channel if family and guests are watching something in your home that unexpectedly becomes offensive or to walk out of the room at someone else's house when something comes on that violates your moral convictions. But it is even more awkward to just sit there during a sexually explicit scene or commercial. It is better to offend family and friends than the Lord.

It Wasn't Always This Way

I used to go to bed with thoughts and images of movies I had just watched lingering in my mind. I would wake up with vivid memories of what I had seen the night before. Much of my time during the day was spent discussing movies and sporting events. Now, most of that seems like such a waste to me.

When I go to bed at night, my thoughts are on the Lord and His Word. When I wake up in the morning, scriptural insight and ministry ideas often flood my mind. Throughout the day the meditations of my heart are focused on the Lord and His faithfulness. The words from my mouth are usually to witness to those who need Christ or to provide encouragement to those who already know Him.

As I said, it wasn't always this way. As I have grown in my relationship with Jesus Christ and renewed my mind with His Word, my perspective and priorities have completely changed.

Now, as I look back over my younger years, I regret the wasted time spent watching, reading, listening, and doing things that took such a negative toll on my life.

Strong Conviction

Watching objectionable movies in the privacy of your home or observing lustful materials while surfing the Internet should be as uncomfortable for a committed believer as sitting in a pornographic movie theater or strip club. As a result, a growing number of Christians are being convicted to remove television and Internet access from their homes or at least strictly monitor them.

My wife received the following letter from a freelance staffer for The 700 Club who filmed our daughter and her husband's testimony for a Valentine's Day special. She wrote:

> It was a joy to meet you in San Diego! Tabitha and Clay did such a terrific job (and Caeleana, too).

When my husband and I were first married, we made a commitment to a "TV free" home for three months. My husband was the driving force behind this. He felt that our time would be better spent talking, praying, reading, or getting out. After three months of no TV, I was sold! Our home is so peaceful and we are able to really enjoy our moments together.

Would the Apostle Paul Own a TV?

In 1999 my son and I traveled for three weeks with a group from Talbot School of Theology as we retraced the steps of the apostle Paul's missionary journeys. Considering the fact that Paul repeatedly warned New Testament believers to abstain from idolatry and sexual immorality, I asked the archeologist and biblical scholar leading the group, "How would the apostle Paul deal with television today?" He responded without hesitation, "The apostle Paul would not have a television in his home."

Most of the programs on television today flaunt the very things Paul told believers to avoid. Likewise, most of the material on television is diametrically opposed to the values and principles God inspired Paul to write about to the New Testament churches.

Besides, Paul was too busy evangelizing his world and making disciples to waste time on unprofitable activities.

It was the apostle Paul who urged the Philippians to let their minds dwell on what is true, noble, right, pure, lovely, admirable, excellent, and praiseworthy. There is no doubt according to Paul's perspective, a believer's home should be filled with the truth of God's Word and praise to the Lord.

Take the TV Challenge

I have challenged many pastors and believers throughout the world to turn off their television for one month. During this month-long fast from television they are to avoid all unnecessary distractions and focus on reading only Scripture and spending time in prayer.

The response has been incredible as countless people have informed me that this was one of the most beneficial times in their lives. It helped them immensely in their walk with the Lord and gave them a whole new perspective.

Why don't you fast from television, movies, and the Internet as you seek the Lord and His Word? Ask the Lord to open your eyes and speak to your heart concerning what He desires for you. Evaluate the programs, movies, web sites, music, magazines, books, and activities that may be pulling you down or diverting your focus from Him. As Hebrews 12:1 encourages—

> ...let us throw off everything that hinders and the sin that so easily entangles....

As I close this chapter on the media connection, I want to make certain you realize what you put in your mind is as crucial as what you keep out. So fill your mind with positive movies, music, magazines, and activities. Like food, do not just avoid what is bad for you; enjoy what is healthy and beneficial.

Even Heroes Suffer Consequences
David and Solomon's Sexual Sins Lead to Tragedy

> Sadly, it is commonplace to see on the news powerful political and religious leaders fall from their lofty positions as a result of sexual immorality. These people discard everything they have labored for in exchange for extramarital sex. Why is it so many people throw away their reputation, family, career and dignity for a few moments of physical pleasure?
> —Lieutenant Colonel Douglas V. Mastriano

David and Solomon provide crucial lessons for us—as pertinent as they were three millennia ago. David was a man after God's heart. He desired to obey the Lord's commandments and honor Him. Yet, David had a serious character weakness—a lust for women.

We all are aware of David's grievous transgression when he committed adultery with Bathsheba and then had her husband put to death. We also know that God sent Nathan the prophet to rebuke David and to pronounce judgment against him.

In Psalm 51 we read about David's sincere repentance. You can almost feel David's emotions through the verses of this psalm. God forgave and restored David, but there were some tragic consequences, as there will be in the lives and families of those who do not learn from David's failure.

New Year's Eve in Rome

Consequences of sin often occur swiftly and unexpectedly—as happened to me while on a ministry trip in Rome one New Year's Eve. My son and another seminary student went with me to the Forum, where they were having a massive gathering. We wanted to see how the Romans celebrate New Year's Eve, so about 10:00 p.m. we started on a 30-minute walk from our hotel. Firecrackers were being thrown throughout the night—many at people's feet as they passed by.

As we walked through a park, a bottle rocket was shot into the trees overhead. Suddenly we heard a thunderous sound. It was the flapping wings of thousands of large black birds as they began to take off from the branches in panic. The sky overhead turned pitch black from the mass of birds blocking out the light from the moon and the stars. It suddenly occurred to me what thousands of panicked birds do, so I told those with me to run for cover. Before we could get to shelter we began to be bombarded by bird droppings. We quickly put the hoods of our coats up as we ran to a nearby shelter—getting hit many times on the way.

Messing with illicit sex is like shooting a bottle rocket into trees loaded with thousands of birds. Panic will ensue as you are pelted with the consequences. You may think you are getting away with sexual sin when suddenly the peaceful calm unexpectedly erupts into chaos. Eventually, as the Bible says, we reap what we sow as our sins are exposed.

One or more of the following consequences will begin to pelt you like bird droppings:

- Sexually transmitted diseases
- Pregnancy (with options of abortion, adoption, or keeping the baby)
- Guilt, shame, disgust
- Fear (of getting caught, STDs, or pregnant)
- Terror and tears (when you do get caught)

- Struggle with immoral thoughts and lustful memories of past escapades for the rest of your life
- Ensnared in deception and lies
- Loss of trust and intimacy (hard for partner to give themselves totally to someone they do not trust)
- Loss of happiness, peace, and joy
- Stress
- Premature aging
- Wasted time and potential
- Emotional and spiritual problems
- Tarnished testimony
- Dishonoring the Lord and bringing reproach on His name
- Damaged or ruined marriages
- Hurt and devastated children

A friend I had not seen for many years told me that he believed in God. He explained that he had done everything the Bible told him not to do, and suffered all the consequences. He knew there must be a God to inspire such an accurate Book.

Remember the female prisoner you read about in chapter two? How about all the tragic stories in chapter one? Countless other lives—both male and female, young and old—have been marred or ruined because of ignoring God's warnings concerning promiscuity and sexual immorality.

Consequences Overwhelm David

David's failure to control his desire for women caused much suffering for him and his family. After his adulterous sin with Bathsheba, one calamity after another entered his life. David's reputation was forever tarnished. He suffered violence, strife, and sorrow the remaining 25 years of his life.

David's illegitimate baby died. One of his sons, Amnon, raped his half-sister, Tamar. Although David was king, he probably felt powerless to deal with Amnon because of his own previous sin with Bathsheba. Then another son of David,

Absalom, killed Amnon for raping his sister. Absalom later led a rebellion against David, forcing David to flee Jerusalem. Absalom even lay with his father's concubines in broad daylight in the sight of all Israel. Then this rebellious son was put to death against David's wishes. Even as David was dying, another son, Adonijah, tried to set himself up as king when Solomon was the appointed one. Adonijah was later executed by Solomon.

All these tragedies stem from that time when he disobeyed the Lord and sinned with Bathsheba. So learn a lesson from David and do not allow the enticements of sin or the pleasures of this world to lure you away from pure devotion to Christ. Only a fool thinks he can play with fire and not get burned. Eventually the consequences will overtake you as unexpectedly and as swiftly as those birds did us in Rome.

David's Advice to Solomon

Near the end of David's life, he wisely admonished his son—

And you, my son Solomon, acknowledge the God of your father, and serve Him with wholehearted devotion and with a willing mind, for the Lord searches every heart and understands every motive behind the thoughts. If you seek Him, He will be found by you; but if you forsake Him, He will reject you forever (1 Chronicles 28:9).

David also told Solomon—

I am about to go the way of all the earth, so be strong, show yourself a man, and observe what the Lord your God requires: Walk in His ways...so that you may prosper in all you do and wherever you go (1 Kings 2:2, 3).

Even Heroes Suffer Consequences

Solomon started his reign by heeding David's advice. He honored the Lord and obeyed His commands. The Lord gave Solomon great wisdom, enabled him to build the Temple in Jerusalem, and inspired him to write many proverbs. However, something went wrong. We see that the end of Solomon's life is not as glorious as the beginning. What happened?

Like his father, Solomon had a great lust for women. Scripture reveals that Solomon loved many foreign women. He had 700 wives of royal birth and 300 concubines.

Solomon took wives from nations which God had forbidden the Israelites to intermarry with because God knew they would turn the hearts of His people after their gods. When Solomon became king, he was admonished to obey the Lord's commands. As king he was supposed to read the Law all the days of his life to ensure he carefully followed all the words of the Lord.

Solomon knew the Law and initially read it often. He was aware that God prohibited marrying pagan wives so his heart would not be led astray and knew God would not tolerate idolatry.

Looking back, we may wonder how the wisest man in the world could become so foolish. But like many today, Solomon did not heed God's warnings. He allowed lust and compromise to erode his commitment to the God of the Bible.

I am sure Solomon began to read less and less the commands of the Law—if at all. Instead of trusting the Lord, Solomon made alliances with the nations around him. He married many foreign wives who led him astray.

As Solomon became influenced by his foreign wives, a transition happened. Instead of wholeheartedly serving the Lord, Solomon tolerated the paganism of his foreign wives. He even built high places for them to burn incense and offer sacrifices to their gods. Solomon's heart was turned after their gods and he participated in their immoral and idolatrous rituals—setting a devastating pattern for Israel's future kings for generations to come.

Spiritual Adultery

Sexual immorality usually leads to spiritual adultery—as it did in Solomon's case. First Kings chapter 11:1-14 gives an overview of this sad scenario—

> King Solomon, however, loved many foreign women.... They were from nations about which the Lord had told the Israelites, "You must not intermarry with them, because they will surely turn your hearts after their gods." Nevertheless, Solomon held fast to them in love...and his wives led him astray. As Solomon grew old, his wives turned his heart after other gods, and his heart was not fully devoted to the Lord his God, as the heart of David his father had been. He followed Ashtoreth the goddess of the Sidonians, and Molech the detestable god of the Ammonites. So Solomon did evil in the eyes of the Lord; he did not follow the Lord completely, as David his father had done. On a hill east of Jerusalem, Solomon built a high place for Chemosh the detestable god of Moab, and for Molech the detestable god of the Ammonites. He did the same for all his foreign wives, who burned incense and offered sacrifices to their gods.
>
> The Lord became angry with Solomon because his heart had turned away from the Lord, the God of Israel, who had appeared to him twice. Although He had forbidden Solomon to follow other gods, Solomon did not keep the Lord's command. So the Lord said to Solomon, "Since this is your attitude and you have not kept My covenant and My decrees, which I commanded you, I will most certainly tear the kingdom away from you and give it to one of your subordinates. Nevertheless, for the sake of

David your father, I will not do it during your lifetime. I will tear it out of the hand of your son. Yet I will not tear the whole kingdom from him, but will give him one tribe for the sake of David My servant and for the sake of Jerusalem, which I have chosen." Then the Lord raised up against Solomon an adversary....

Solomon's lust for women led to his downfall. If only he and his father David would have heeded God's Word given through Moses hundreds of years earlier, their tragic consequences could have been avoided.

Seduced by Sex

When Moses was leading the Israelites out of Egyptian bondage, Balak, king of Moab, wanted Balaam to curse Israel. However, God would not allow this. So what did Balaam tell Balak to do? He told him to seduce Israel into sexual immorality and idolatry so the hand of the Lord would be against them (Numbers 31:16). As a result, the Moabites turned many Israelites away from the Lord by enticing them into spiritual harlotry through the sensual worship of their gods.

Numbers 25:1-3 (NAS) states—

While Israel remained at Shittim, the people began to play the harlot with the daughters of Moab. For they invited the people to the sacrifices of their gods, and the people ate and bowed down to their gods. So Israel joined themselves to Baal of Peor, and the Lord was angry against Israel.

Enticed by the Moabite women, the Israelite men participated in the sexual rituals of Baal worship and bowed down and offered sacrifice to their gods. Soon God's judgment was meted out for Israel's disobedience and rebellion.

No wonder when the apostles and elders held a council in Jerusalem to determine what should be required of the new Gentile converts, they advised them to abstain from food sacrificed to idols and from sexual immorality (Acts 15:20). Idolatry and sexual immorality, more than anything else in Scripture, have caused God's people to fall.

In His rebuke of the Church in Pergamum near the end of the first century A.D., the resurrected and glorified Christ said—

> *I have a few things against you: You have people there who hold to the teaching of Balaam, who taught Balak to entice the Israelites to sin by eating food sacrificed to idols and by committing sexual immorality* (Revelation 2:14).

What do you think Christ is saying to the Church today? Repent of your sexual immorality and idolatry before judgment is meted out against you.

Do Not Despise the Lord—Be Faithful

When David sinned with Bathsheba, Nathan said to him, "Why did you despise the word of the Lord by doing what is evil in His eyes?" (2 Samuel 12:9). "Despise" (Hebrew *bazah*) means to treat contemptuously, to scorn, to make of little account. We despise God's Word and dishonor Him when we live a lifestyle or participate in practices contrary to His will.

What does virtually every married person want in a relationship? Faithfulness! God desires the same in our relationship with Him. His love and faithfulness should compel us to faithfulness. We should be grieved when He is dishonored or any reproach is brought upon His name.

Solomon's Final Lesson

Although Solomon had tremendous wealth, power, wisdom, and many beautiful women, it did not satisfy him. After having and trying everything imaginable, the last few verses of Ecclesiastes sum up what Solomon learned the hard way—

> *Now all has been heard; here is the conclusion of the matter: Fear God and keep His commandments, for this is the whole duty of man. For God will bring every deed into judgment, including every hidden thing, whether it is good or evil* (Ecclesiastes 12:13-14).

Both Sides of Life

I discovered the same dead-end reality as Solomon. In my foolishness before I knew the Lord I tried almost everything imaginable. But true and long-lasting peace and fulfillment eluded me. The only solution to my dilemma was to give my life to Jesus Christ.

I know both sides of life—from being totally out of control in virtually every aspect of my life, to bringing every aspect of my life under control with the Lord's help. He is a merciful, loving, and forgiving God who not only set me free, but brought about a tremendous transformation and victory in my life.

Navy Seal Set Free

While ministering at a men's retreat, I met a Chief Instructor for Navy Seals, Marines, and junior officers. He was also a deacon and men's leader at church.

Following my first message he asked to see my notes on the four things I mentioned that people will not repent of during the Tribulation. After I read the Scriptures to him he looked at me and said, "I am guilty of all four." He methodically continued, "I am a liar and a thief because I steal from work. I am proud and therefore an idolater. I am a murderer because I kill people with my words. And I am sexually immoral because I am in a four-year affair that no one knows about except me, her, the Lord, and now you."

After telling me he is a Christian and married with three children, I read Ephesians 5:1-13 to him. I then asked him, "If you were forced to watch your daughter being raped and tortured, would you still want to have sex with this other woman?" He shook his head no. I said, "It would never even enter your mind. You see, it is all perspective."

I told him that unless he repented, these sins would consume him like a cancer. His illicit sexual relationship would destroy him physically, mentally, and spiritually, as well as destroy his marriage and hurt his children. "It is eating me up," he said as he showed me a rash on his arm. "I have to get rid of this anguish I am under."

He dropped to his knees and repented. After we prayed he told me that the reason God changed my schedule to be at this men's retreat this weekend, instead of ministering in Germany on U.S. military bases as previously planned, was so he could hear me speak. Otherwise, he would have never dealt with these issues in his life.

The next day as I was preparing to leave after my closing message, he came up to me and said that he was finally free.

I wish I could say that all went well with him and his wife. Although he ended the relationship with the other woman, his past unfaithfulness triggered tremendous fallout in his marriage and family that surpassed any rigors he faced in becoming a Navy Seal. Nevertheless, the Lord has forgiven him and he learned the wisdom of obeying Scripture and seeking to be a true "warrior for Christ."

An important lesson for all of us to learn is that even all the strength, discipline, and determination of a Navy Seal is insufficient to avert sexual temptation. We must be motivated to obey God's Word and rely on the Lord to strengthen us in our weakness. This battle is too strong to fight and win without His help.

Do You Love Me More Than These?

Three times Peter denied knowing the Lord as Jesus was being interrogated before the High Priest. Then Peter ran away and abandoned Him and wept bitterly.

Several days after the crucifixion, the resurrected Christ was having breakfast with His disciples on the shore of the Sea of Galilee. He asked Peter a probing question, "Do you truly love Me more than these?" (John 21:15).

Jesus' question to Peter was not in reference to a sexual failure. But how would you answer a similar question if the Lord asked you, "Do you truly love Me more than pornography and illicit sexual relationships?"

I hope you will be able to respond with the same words and conviction of Peter, "Yes Lord, You know I do." And then, like Peter, live the rest of your life demonstrating that conviction.

Day after day and night after night we must shut down thoughts and behaviors that cause us to deny and abandon our Lord.

God's Perspective

If there is a God—and I am convinced there is—then we need to live according to His guidelines and requirements. As our Creator, He knows what is best for us. Following His advice safeguards us from suffering needless immediate, long-term, and eternal consequences.

The Holy Bible speaks in a timely fashion concerning the full spectrum of sexuality. In this chapter, we will examine more of what Scripture has to say.

A strong warning is given in 2 Peter 2:2-19 concerning false teachers who live in immorality. Excerpts follow—

> *Many follow their shameful ways and bring the way of truth into disrepute. Their idea of pleasure is to carouse in broad daylight. With eyes full of adultery, they never stop sinning. They seduce the unstable by appealing to the lustful desires of sinful human nature. They promise freedom, while they themselves are slaves of depravity— for a man is a slave to whatever has mastered him.*

The flirtations of an immoral woman may seem enticing, but keep Solomon's warning in mind—

> *Do not lust in your heart after her beauty or let her captivate you with her eyes. Can a man scoop fire into*

his lap without his clothes being burned? So is he who sleeps with another man's wife; no one who touches her will go unpunished. A man who commits adultery lacks judgment; whoever does so destroys himself. Blows and disgrace are his lot, and his shame will never be wiped away (Proverbs 6:25-33).

Proverbs chapter 7 cautions concerning the seductive power of the adulteress. Excerpts follow—

My son, keep my commands and you will live; guard my teachings as the apple of your eye. Bind them on your fingers; write them on your heart. They will keep you from the adulteress, from the wayward wife with her seductive words.

I saw among the simple, I noticed among the young men, a youth who lacked judgment. He was going down the street near her corner, walking along in the direction of her house at twilight, as the dark of night set in.

Then out came a woman to meet him, dressed like a prostitute and with crafty intent. She took hold of him and kissed him and said: "I looked for you and have found you! I have covered my bed with colored linens. Come, let's drink deep of love till morning; let's enjoy ourselves with love! My husband is not at home; he has gone on a long journey."

With persuasive words she led him astray; she seduced him with her smooth talk. All at once he followed her like an ox going to the slaughter, like a bird darting into a snare, little knowing it will cost him his life.

Now then, my sons, listen to me; pay attention to what I say. Do not let your heart turn to her ways or stray into her paths. Many are the victims she has brought down; her slain are a mighty throng. Her house is a highway to the grave, leading down to the chambers of death.

No wonder that in Ecclesiastes 7:26 Solomon wrote—

I find more bitter than death the woman who is a snare, whose heart is a trap and whose hands are chains. The man who pleases God will escape her, but the sinner she will ensnare.

We learned from the previous chapter that Solomon did not follow his own advice and suffered dire consequences. Solomon is an example of the dilemma of life: knowing what to do but not doing it.

Let me also emphasize that the warnings in Scripture are relevant for both sexes. One gender does not have a monopoly on sinful or seductive behavior.

The apostle Paul admonishes us in 1 Corinthians 6:18—

Flee from sexual immorality. All other sins a man commits are outside his body, but he who sins sexually sins against his own body.

Hebrews 13:4 clearly states—

Marriage should be honored by all, and the marriage bed kept pure, for God will judge the adulterer and all the sexually immoral.

Revelation 2:20-22 was written to a first century church in Thyatira, but is a warning to all believers—

I have this against you: You tolerate that woman Jezebel, who calls herself a prophetess. By her teaching she misleads my servants into sexual immorality....

I have given her time to repent of her immorality, but she is unwilling. So I will cast her on a bed of suffering, and I will make those who commit adultery with her suffer intensely, unless they repent of her ways.

The original Jezebel (in the Old Testament) is not known to have committed any sexual sins. Her distinguishing sin was promoting false gods. But by identifying this woman in Thyatira with the wicked Jezebel of the Old Testament, the Lord is making a close link between sexual sin and idolatry.

Ephesians 5:3-5 makes it crystal clear—

But among you there must not be even a hint of sexual immorality, or of any kind of impurity...these are improper for God's holy people. Nor should there be obscenity, foolish talk or coarse joking.... For of this you can be sure: No immoral, impure or greedy person—such a man is an idolater—has any inheritance in the kingdom of Christ and of God.

Unlawful Sexual Relations

The Law given to Moses discloses various aspects of sexual activity that God forbids. An overview follows—

No one is to approach any close relative to have sexual relations. Do not have sexual relations with your mother. Do not have sexual relations with your father's wife. Do not have sexual relations with your sister.... Do not have sexual relations with your son's daughter or your daughter's daughter.

Do not have sexual relations with your father's sister. Do not have sexual relations with your mother's sister. Do not dishonor your father's brother by approaching his wife to have sexual relations; she is your aunt. Do not have sexual relations with your daughter-in-law. Do not have sexual relations with your brother's wife.

Do not have sexual relations with both a woman and her daughter. Do not have sexual relations with either her son's daughter or her daughter's daughter; they are her close relatives. That is wickedness. Do not take your wife's sister as a rival wife and have sexual relations with her while your wife is living. Do not approach a woman to have sexual relations during the uncleanness of her monthly period. Do not have sexual relations with your neighbor's wife and defile yourself with her.

Do not lie with a man as one lies with a woman; that is detestable. Do not have sexual relations with an animal and defile yourself with it. A woman must not present herself to an animal to have sexual relations with it; that is a perversion.

Do not defile yourselves in any of these ways, because this is how the nations that I am going to drive out before you became defiled. Keep my requirements and do not follow any of the detestable customs that were practiced before you came and do not defile yourselves with them. I am the LORD your God (Leviticus 18:6-30).

Honor God with Your Body

Scriptures reflecting the call to honor the Lord with our bodies and live godly lives are plentiful. The following are just a few.

First Corinthians 6:13-20—

> ...The body is not meant for sexual immorality, but for the Lord.... Do you not know that your bodies are members of Christ Himself? Shall I then take the members of Christ and unite them with a prostitute?

Never!...Do you not know that your body is a temple of the Holy Spirit, who is in you, whom you have received from God? You are not your own; you were bought at a price. Therefore honor God with your body.

Romans 13:13,14—

Let us behave decently, as in the daytime, not in orgies and drunkenness, not in sexual immorality and debauchery, not in dissension and jealousy. Rather, clothe yourselves with the Lord Jesus Christ, and do not think about how to gratify the desires of the sinful nature.

Second Peter 3:11,12—

...You ought to live holy and godly lives as you look forward to the day of God and speed its coming....

First John 3:2,3—

Dear friends, now we are children of God, and what we will be has not yet been made known. But we know that when He appears, we shall be like Him, for we shall see Him as He is. Everyone who has this hope in Him purifies himself, just as He is pure.

First Thessalonians 4:3-7—

It is God's will that you should be sanctified: that you should avoid sexual immorality; that each of you should learn to control his own body in a way that is holy and honorable, not in passionate lust like the heathen, who do not know God; and that in this matter no one should wrong his brother or take advantage of him. The Lord will punish men for all such sins, as we have already told you and warned you. For God did not call us to be impure, but to live a holy life.

Sexual Immorality Defined

Comments on Hebrews 13:4 from *The Full Life Study Bible* are insightful—

> Biblical terms used for sexual immorality, describing the breadth of its evil, are as follows: sexual immorality (Greek *porneia*) describes a wide variety of sexual activities before or outside of marriage; it is not limited to consummated sexual acts. Any intimate sexual activity or play outside the marriage relationship, including the touching of the intimate parts of the body or seeing another person's nakedness, is included in this term and is clearly a transgression of God's moral standards for His people (1 Corinthians 6:18; 1 Thessalonians 4:3).
>
> Debauchery, or sensuality, (Greek *aselgeia*) denotes the absence of clear moral principles, especially disregard of sexual self-control that maintains pure behavior. It includes the inclination toward indulging in or arousing sinful lust, and thus is a participation in biblically unjustifiable conduct (Galatians 5:19; Ephesians 4:19; 1 Peter 4:3; 2 Peter 2:2,18).
>
> Exploiting or taking advantage of someone (Greek *pleonekteo*) means to deprive another of the moral purity that God desires for that person in order to satisfy one's own self-centered desires. To arouse in another person sexual desires that cannot be righteously fulfilled is to exploit or take advantage of that person.

Lust (Greek *epithumia*) is having an immoral desire that one would fulfill if the opportunity arose (Ephesians 4:19,22; 1 Peter 4:3; 2 Peter 2:18).

Do Not Deprive Your Mate

As we conclude this chapter on God's perspective, let me mention that spouses who purposely deprive their mates of sexual satisfaction and fulfillment are also violating clear scriptural mandates. First Corinthians 7:3-5 states—

The husband should fulfill his marital duty to his wife, and likewise the wife to her husband. The wife's body does not belong to her alone but also to her husband. In the same way, the husband's body does not belong to him alone but also to his wife. Do not deprive each other except by mutual consent and for a time, so that you may devote yourselves to prayer. Then come together again so that Satan will not tempt you because of your lack of self-control.

God's Intended Design

God did not design male and female for the distorted reality we see today. Instead of men using women merely for pleasure and abusing them, they should be their protectors. Instead of women enticing and coercing men by offering sexual favors, they should maintain their dignity and purity.

Husbands should not demand or force submission by their wives, but should selflessly and sacrificially give of themselves for them. Husbands should treat their wives as precious, delicate jewels, entrusted to their care.

Wives should not manipulate and control their husbands, striving to be the head of the house, but willingly and lovingly submit as to the Lord. Women were not created to be "hurt mates" who undermine and oppose what the Lord wants to do through their husbands, but "help mates" who support and encourage them.

The Lord intends for a man to unconditionally love and protect his wife, and for a wife to be a loyal companion and help mate—both remaining faithful to the Lord and each other. Scripture has a clear and emphatic message for both wives and husbands—

> *Wives, submit to your husbands as to the Lord. For the husband is the head of the wife as Christ is the head of the church, His body, of which He is the Savior. Now as the church submits to Christ, so also wives should submit to their husbands in everything. Husbands, love your wives, just as Christ loved the church and gave Himself up for her. However, each one of you must love his wife as he loves himself, and the wife must respect her husband* (Ephesians 5:22-25,33).

We cannot deny the obvious teaching of Scripture nor the inherent wisdom and blessings when both husband and wife submit to the Lord and honor Him with their lives and marriage.

Steps to Overcoming Sexual Immorality

While ministering in Trinidad in the West Indies I visited their main tourist attraction: a large lake of tar. They claim it is the largest natural pitch deposit in the world (pitch is a black, sticky substance formed in the distillation of coal tar). The guide there offered us a free walk out onto the tar. He assured us he would carefully lead us so we would not fall in. I was warned by my host before, however, that once someone ventures out with him and is ready to come back he says to them, "That will be twenty dollars." He always gets his price from those who walk out with him because only he knows where it is safe to step so you do not fall into the tar pit. It is the same way with sexual immorality—easy to get into, but difficult to get out, and there is always a price to pay.

Understand That Immorality Has a High Price

I warned a pastor who was ensnared in a sexual affair if he continued, he would pay a heavy price. It would cost him his health, emotional stability, spiritual life, finances, and family. That other person may seem fun for the moment, but she is not worth your wife and your life.

I told him he needed the fear of God and if he even had a glimpse of the holiness and awesomeness of God, he would have such fear and respect that he would get on his knees and cry out in repentance. He eventually did. Today, by the grace of God, he is a restored man.

Forgiveness Is Available

Many have made mistakes regarding sexual behavior and failed to obey God's Word, but no matter what you have done or thought, there is hope. Jesus said to the woman caught in adultery, "Neither do I condemn you. Go now and leave your life of sin" (John 8:11).

Knowing believers still make mistakes, the apostle John wrote—

If we confess our sins, He is faithful and just and will forgive us our sins and purify us from all unrighteousness (1 John 1:9).

The correct response to sexual sin, or any sin for that matter, is to confess it to the Lord and receive His forgiveness. True repentance means to turn away from it. Also, be willing to accept any adverse consequences without bitterness or rebellion.

Distressed in Spirit

A Christian man in his thirties said to me, "It is impossible to escape the corruption of this world." I responded, "You can be distressed by it like Lot who lived in degenerate Sodom." We read he was—

…a righteous man, who was distressed by the filthy lives of lawless men for that righteous man, living among them day after day, was tormented in his righteous soul by the lawless deeds he saw and heard (2 Peter 2:7,8).

The Lord can change our hearts and perspective so instead of finding pleasure in scenes of immorality shown on television, movies, and cell phones, or displayed in pornographic literature and web sites, we will be distressed in spirit.

When we see immorality through the eyes of our Creator and comprehend the evil and destruction it unleashes against our spouse, children, ourselves, and society, the perversions being spewed out of immoral cesspools should disgust us—not entertain us.

Ask the Lord to help you look at immorality through His eyes and see His perspective. Ask Him to give you revulsion for illicit sex, but to show you the beauty of marital sex.

The Dynamics of Marital Sex

Illicit sex is usually superficial. In spite of unlimited postures and techniques, it is limited to a shallow physical level.

Marital sex involves physical, mental, and spiritual dimensions. Its dynamics are complex and exciting—too challenging for those who settle for less.

Making love is not just the consummation of a physical act but the compilation of many factors. Faith, love, trust, and commitment are crucial concepts in a marital relationship. What happens throughout the day such as holding hands, walking in the park together, sharing each others trials and joys, speaking kind words instead of nasty or degrading comments, also contributes to the physical, emotional, and spiritual pleasure of marital sex.

Flee from Lust

Every day we face temptations. Opportunities arise in which we can either inflame or suppress our lusts. The choices we make will either enslave or liberate us.

Wisdom admonishes us to follow the advice of 2 Timothy 2:22 (KJV) to "Flee youthful lusts." Before the situation gets out of control—STOP! Think about the consequences and how foolish it would be to proceed.

Learn to say NO! When a guy or girl pressures you to have sex or compromise your beliefs, just say, "No! It violates my convictions. Besides, it is not safe, wise, loving, or fulfilling. I will not risk the consequences. I will wait until marriage."

Titus 2:11-14 states—

For the grace of God that brings salvation has appeared to all men. It teaches us to say "No" to ungodliness and worldly passions, and to live self-controlled, upright and godly lives in this present age, while we wait for the blessed hope—the glorious appearing of our great God and Savior, Jesus Christ, who gave Himself for us to redeem us from all wickedness and to purify for Himself a people that are His very own, eager to do what is good.

Today, fleeing youthful lusts also means avoiding movies, music, magazines, and web sites, as well as people, who sexually entice.

Depend on the Spirit of God to give you the wisdom and self-control to resist the temptation and to flee the scene if necessary—like Joseph, who escaped the sexual advances of Potiphar's wife—

Now Joseph was well-built and handsome, and after a while his master's wife took notice of Joseph and said, "Come to bed with me!" But he refused..."My master has withheld nothing from me except you, because you are his wife. How then could I do such a wicked thing and sin against God?" And though she spoke to Joseph day after day, he refused to go to bed with her or even be with her. One day he went into the house to attend to his duties, and none of the household servants was inside. She caught him by his cloak and said, "Come to bed with me!" But he left his cloak in her hand and ran out of the house (Genesis 39:6-12).

That's as Far as I Go

If you see an attractive person and your mind begins to take you in a direction it should not, or if certain sights, sounds, smells, and circumstances unexpectedly transport you back to memories and habits, stop and say to yourself something such as, "No! That's not what I want. This is as far as I go. I choose You, Lord."

Instead of being entertained by lewd conduct and allowing it to enter your heart, or before overstepping verbal, emotional, or physical boundaries, leading to an illicit relationship, stop and say something like, "No! It is not going to happen. That leads to death. It will destroy me. I choose You, Lord."

It is amazing how our thoughts and emotions respond to an assertive affirmation. These types of reinforcements will greatly help your resolve to not fall into old ruts and patterns, but to keep your thoughts and behavior pure before the Lord.

Someone wisely said, "Lord, when I have the desire, take away the opportunity. And when I have the opportunity, take away the desire."

Guard Your Life and Home

I used to do self-defense clinics in schools and for other groups where I demonstrated how to avoid potential confrontations and how to deal with attack situations. "But the most important principle," I would tell the students, "is to use wisdom in avoiding places, people, and situations where you know a confrontation or an attack is likely to occur."

Likewise, to overcome sexual immorality, you must avoid places, people, and situations that will lead you into temptation. Avoid compromising circumstances that are conducive to leading you into lust and immorality. Take steps to guard your life and your home by removing or limiting television, putting a filter on your computer, and so on.

Avoid setting yourself up for temptation. Randomly surfing the Internet, flicking through television channels, or browsing at a book store will more than likely flash some enticing visuals before your eyes that will lead to another defeat if you are not wise in escaping them and strong in overcoming them.

Being in your bedroom or the back seat of a car in a remote area with someone to whom you are physically attracted is like playing Russian roulette. Sooner or later the gun will fire. No matter how pure your intentions, you are setting yourself up for defeat by violating the biblical mandate—"Flee youthful lusts!"

First Thessalonians 5:22 (KJV) admonishes us to "abstain from all appearance of evil."

Why Am I Being Defeated?

As a new Christian I used to think, "Lord, I am going to put myself in the midst of every temptation so I can prove how powerful You are in enabling me to overcome them." I wondered why I was often being defeated.

The Lord made me mindful of when the children of Israel entered and conquered the promised land. God told them to destroy all the idols and high places and often either to kill all the men, women, and children or to drive them out (Exodus 34:11-13; Deuteronomy 7:1-5).

At first I thought this was cruel. I thought it revealed a weakness in Him—that He was unable to preserve His people in the midst of temptation. But the Lord knows the attraction and enticement of sin. He gives us wisdom to avoid temptation before it ensnares, enslaves, and destroys us—just as it did to the Israelites on numerous occasions when they violated His commands.

Jesus knew how important it is to deal with and remove our source of temptation. He said—

> *If your hand or your foot causes you to sin, cut it off and throw it away. It is better for you to enter life maimed or crippled than to have two hands or two feet*

and be thrown into eternal fire. And if your eye causes you to sin, gouge it out and throw it away. It is better for you to enter life with one eye than to have two eyes and be thrown into the fire of hell (Matthew 18:8,9).

Jesus does not mean for us to do this literally. If that were so, the disciples and New Testament believers would all have been maimed and crippled. Rather, He was emphasizing the importance of using wisdom in removing and avoiding sources of temptation and sin.

Stand persistently on 1 Corinthians 10:13, which promises—

No temptation has seized you except what is common to man. And God is faithful; He will not let you be tempted beyond what you can bear. But when you are tempted, He will also provide a way out so that you can stand up under it.

However, do not purposely place yourself in a tempting situation and expect this principle to rescue you. This is tempting the Lord and flirting with disaster.

On the other hand, if you do sin, quickly go before the Lord, our great High Priest, and confess your sin. Hebrews 4:14-16 will be a comfort and encouragement—

…since we have a great high priest who has gone through the heavens, Jesus the Son of God, let us hold firmly to the faith we profess. For we do not have a high priest who is unable to sympathize with our weaknesses, but we have one who has been tempted in every way, just as we are—yet was without sin. Let us then approach the throne of grace with confidence, so that we may receive mercy and find grace to help us in our time of need.

Determine in Advance

Something else I told the female students when I taught self-defense clinics was they must determine in advance whether they would submit to rape or risk their life resisting. I warned them once the emotions of an attack situation occur, they would not have time to think through their options rationally, but would probably react in panic unless they had a predetermined response.

So, too, we must determine in advance what we will or will not do concerning sexual activity. If you do not do so, and you find yourself in a tempting situation such as walking past a porn shop or alone with an attractive and available person as music plays softly in the background creating the perfect atmosphere, you will be defeated. The emotions of sensual allurement under these kind of circumstances are incredibly strong.

However, if you have determined in your heart in advance concerning what you will not do, and made a commitment to the Lord by setting limits regarding what you will do, then you have a much better chance to resist temptation.

Realize, a temptation to sin can also, by resistance, be a test and opportunity to prove your obedience to the Lord and make you a more effective witness. Not that you should be hunting for tests; they will find you in some of the most unexpected ways and places.

What a great emotional feeling it is to walk away from temptation. The sense of victory will ultimately prove far better than if you gave in. Each conquest over sexual sin makes you stronger and creates an exhilarating sense of being free.

A Lesson from Seminary Graduates

While working on his master's degree at Talbot Theological Seminary, my son BJ, learned some helpful insights in a chapel service to help believers guard themselves from sexual temptations. He relates the following summation and recommendations—

A study based on 200 male seminary graduates who had fallen prey to sexual immorality revealed there were four traits missing in the lives of these men.

#1. These men did not spend personal time with God. They lacked an intimate prayer and devotional life. Perhaps, because of the demands of their ministry, these men felt they simply did not have time to pray and study God's Word.

However, to avoid sexual temptations, we must meditate daily upon God's Word (Joshua 1:8; Matthew 4:4), and live a life of continual prayer (Colossians 4:2). Regardless of our busy schedules, we should never neglect spending time with God. These "holy habits" were a trademark of Jesus' ministry on earth (Matthew 14:23; 26:36-44; Mark 6:46; 14:32; Luke 6:12; 9:28).

#2. These men had no personal accountability in their lives. They tried to live their Christian lives on their own. However, the Christian life is not to be one of isolation, but is lived out within a community of other believers. Every Christian needs the encouragement and edification of other believers. We must have at least one person in our life who loves us enough to encourage us when we are feeling discouraged, and to correct us when we are living in opposition to the standards of God's Word. Seek to fellowship with mature Christians whom you can trust and who will provide you with prayer support, encouragement, accountability, and wise counsel.

#3. Ninety percent of these men got involved in sexual promiscuity by counseling women. To avoid becoming emotionally and/or sexually involved with someone we are counseling or helping, we must not be alone with them. Paul told Titus it is the duty of older women to instruct/encourage younger women (Titus 2:3-5).

This principle goes beyond the confines of counseling, as it demonstrates believers should stay away from inappropriate situations (being alone, "friendly" flirtation, coarse joking, and so on). We should conduct ourselves in a manner reflective of God's holiness as we follow the examples of Joseph (Genesis 39:6-12) and Job (Job 31:1) to flee situations and avoid thoughts that may compromise us.

#4. These men had the attitude they were immune or "too spiritual" to fall prey to the deceptions and lure of sexual immorality. As believers, we need to remain alert because our adversary the devil prowls around like a roaring lion seeking someone to devour (1 Peter 5:8).

We must never think we are exempt from the temptations of sexual immorality. Rather, may we humbly walk every day in the grace of God as we continue to press on toward the goal for the prize of the upward call of God in Christ Jesus (Philippians 3:14).

Evaluate All Things and Be Discerning

Entertainment does more than entertain. It conveys ideas, values, philosophies, and lifestyles. That is why it is imperative you evaluate television, movies, music, the Internet, books, and magazines with a discerning mind and heart.

When you are exposed to something enticing and lustful, do not be like a sponge soaking it up and letting it enter your heart. Instead, be like a filter and evaluate everything you watch, read, and listen to by considering its immediate and long-term implications. Let what is not true and beneficial be like water rolling off the back of a duck. Do not let it take root in your heart. Say to yourself, "This visual representation or message content is not truth and reality. It is not what I want. I choose to honor You, Lord."

We Are All Exposed

Whether you are at the beach, at work, watching television, listening to the news, using your computer, driving down the road, walking at the mall, or even sitting in the pew, there are constant sources of temptation. We are all exposed. Just checking e-mails or text messages can result in a host of unwanted sexual words and images.

Billboards, advertisements, magazines, books, movies, music, the Internet, and scantily clad people constantly stimulate the mind toward sexual thoughts and temptations. It is only by the grace of God anyone survives unscathed in this sex-oriented society.

Everyone has sexual thoughts and temptations. What you do with those thoughts and temptations determines whether it is merely a "temptation to sin" or actual "adultery in your heart."

In Matthew 15:19 Christ reveals sin begins in the heart. He states, "For out of the heart come evil thoughts, murder, adultery, sexual immorality...."

Lust Defined

The lust Jesus referred to is when you look with the attitude that, given the opportunity, you would participate with someone other than your spouse in such things as intimate conversations, hugging, kissing, looking upon their nakedness, or sexual contact of any kind. Once you fantasize that possibility in your mind and condone it in your heart, the actual fulfillment is just a step away.

No wonder Jesus said if you have lust for someone in your heart, you have already committed adultery with him or her. The line that separates giving in or not giving in is determined in our thought life and heart.

Extended eye contact, flirtatious conversation, as well as watching or reading sexually stimulating materials, are sparks which ignite lust and passion, leading to a wildfire of sexual involvement. To avoid adultery in your heart and mind, do not look at anyone except your spouse in contemplation of having sexual intimacy with them.

A married man told me that as he was waiting in a doctor's office he noticed a beautiful woman. Instead of looking her up and down and letting his imagination run wild, he merely acknowledged her attractiveness, then turned his gaze forward and focused his thoughts elsewhere.

Like seeing a 1968 Corvette in mint condition, instead of trying to steal it and take it home with him, he would merely appreciate its design. So, too, if he sees an attractive woman, instead of lusting and trying to pick her up, he merely acknowledges the magnificence of the God who designed her.

Control Your Thoughts

It is obvious that sexual involvements first begin as thoughts in our minds and lust in our hearts. If we are going to overcome the sexual temptations we face in a sexually explicit and uninhibited society, we must control our thoughts and the ensuing emotions.

What you allow your mind to be programmed with will eventually manifest itself in your thoughts, emotions, words, and behavior. Thoughts produce emotions which in turn lead to words and actions. Behavior patterns formulate our lifestyle, which in turn, determines our destiny.

If you fill your mind with garbage, you will develop a filthy thought life and corrupt lifestyle. It is inevitable and only a matter of time. What we watch, read, and listen to does affect us.

Is it any wonder why so many people manifest out-of-control language and behavior? Look at their mental diet.

The Lord has taught me that I must not tolerate certain thoughts. Thoughts of lust, worry, fear, jealousy, bitterness, and greed that come into my mind are intruders that will sap my strength, joy, and peace. They will enslave and destroy me. God says, "Resist them!" Fight against them as though you were fighting against an intruder in your house who was attempting to rape and kill your family.

Second Corinthians 10:5 encourages us to "Take captive every thought to make it obedient to Christ." Romans 12:2 says, "Do not conform any longer to the pattern of this world, but be transformed by the renewing of your mind...."

Psalm 119:9,11 asks and answers a very relevant question, "How can a young man keep his way pure? By living according to Your Word. I have hidden Your Word in my heart that I might not sin against You."

Philippians 4:8 tells us: "Finally, brothers, whatever is true, whatever is noble, whatever is right, whatever is pure, whatever is lovely, whatever is admirable—if anything is excellent or praiseworthy—think about such things."

Those who want mental discipline and victory over sexual immorality will be wise to reflect upon and implement the above biblical principles.

You Can Overcome Immorality

Do not deceive yourself into believing you cannot overcome sexual immorality. You can—and must.

God always has a remnant who faithfully honor Him. Even during the Tribulation period, in the midst of the most vile and corrupt generation in human history, as unrepentant sexual immorality is rampant, there will be many who follow the Lord wholeheartedly. They will keep themselves pure and will not defile themselves with women (Revelation 14:4).

Steps to Immorality or Victory

Seduction to immorality and sin is often a five step procedure: 1) Think it. 2) Dwell on it. 3) Desire it. 4) Do it. 5) Pay for it.

Temptation starts as a thought or a glance. An idea enters your mind. If you do not dismiss it, but dwell on it, you will quickly find yourself desiring it. As soon as the opportunity arises, you will fulfill it. What began as a mere thought, if left unchecked, can lead to a devastating action.

Another set of steps I have discovered, which leads to sexual immorality are:

First, is looking. Not just looking and thinking, "That's an attractive person," but focusing on explicit parts of the body, lusting, fantasizing, and contemplating how to get it. Allowing thoughts to linger on explicit details and dwelling on sexual fantasies will only feed the fire and lead to illicit sexual involvement.

Second, is placing yourself in a situation where something is likely to happen.

Third, is actual involvement in sexual immorality. James 1:14,15 (NAS) says it this way, "But each one is tempted when he is carried away and enticed by his own lust. Then when lust has conceived, it gives birth to sin; and when sin is accomplished, it brings forth death."

Therefore, to be victorious in overcoming sexual immorality, do the following:

First, commit to the Lord that with His help you will not become involved in illicit sexual relationships and promiscuity. Now that you are a Christian, fornication and adultery are no longer an option.

Second, commit to the Lord that with His help, you will not purposely place yourself in a situation where you know something immoral is likely to happen. Nor will you look for someone to become a potential partner in immorality—or even flirt with that intent.

Third, commit to the Lord that with His help you will not look with lust in your heart. You will not focus on explicit details or fantasize. This includes pornography, sexually explicit movies and music, and other erotic materials. Why waste your time looking when you have already determined in your heart that nothing is going to happen?

Look Without Lusting

A Christian woman living in New York City and seeking to live purely before the Lord said to me concerning all the smut-filled news stands: "I have learned to walk keeping my eyes down and looking straight ahead." I think we can all learn from her example.

Job said something similar: "I made a covenant with my eyes not to look lustfully at a girl" (Job 31:1). David asserted, "I will set before my eyes no vile thing" (Psalm 101:3).

Josh McDowell says it this way: "When you see or meet a girl who brings lustful thoughts to mind, force yourself to look into her face and especially her eyes. This will help you to recognize and respond to the real person who is there and not just the body that person is living in."

Learn to look without lusting. Do not look at other people as sexual objects for your selfish gratification, but look at them as someone for whom Christ died. Be more concerned about the condition of their heart than the shape of their body. Be more concerned about their eternal destiny than obtaining a brief glimpse of their anatomy.

Give the Lord Control

Our emotions and bodies may desire something, but we have a will. We can choose to surrender our will to the Lord and give Him control.

One reason why I fast, exercise, and eat nutritiously is to develop discipline and self-control in every area of my life—physically, mentally, and spiritually.

The apostle Paul said—

All things are lawful for me, but not all things are profitable. All things are lawful for me, but I will not be mastered [or controlled] by anything (1 Corinthians 6:12 NAS).

As believers we have freedom in Christ. However, if something controls us, we are no longer free—but slaves to recurring habits and practices.

I do not know about you, but I only want to be controlled by my Lord. I want to bring every aspect of my life under His control and walk in His wisdom, strength, and empowerment.

The Lord has protected and spared my life so many times that I consider myself dead. Therefore, I have no right to pursue sinful desires, but only to seek His will and fulfill His purpose.

Fruit of the Spirit

The choice is yours—you will either be controlled by the lust of the flesh or the fruit of the Spirit. Self-control is a fruit of the Spirit (Galatians 5:22,23), not of will power. If you try to do it merely in your own strength and with self-effort, you will be continually defeated and frustrated.

You must allow God's Spirit to bring your life under control. He will help you apply the biblical principles I have been sharing with you in this book.

We draw closer to the Lord when we read His Word daily and desire His Spirit to control our lives. As we choose to obey His Word, we are conformed more and more into His likeness. The fruit of His Spirit is developed in our lives and we are empowered to walk in victory.

Ask the Lord for Help

When I first started this ministry, the Lord spoke to my heart that He would greatly use and bless me if I remained faithful. He also warned that sexual immorality would destroy me, if I let it get a foothold in my life. Because of this, whenever I spend time in fasting and prayer, I ask the Lord to burn any lust out of my life and help me by His Spirit to overcome it.

I strive to live as one who will one day give an account to the Lord for my thoughts, words, and actions. No temporary affair or sexual addiction is worth my Lord, my family, my ministry, and my health.

In my desire to live a pure life before the Lord, my prayer is—

Forgive me and help me by Your Spirit to overcome sexual immorality and lust. Help me never to forget how You have dealt with me or the consequences of David, Solomon, and Samson. Also, help me never to forget what You have taught me: to look at everyone through Your eyes—someone for whom You died, not someone to be used for selfish gratification; to walk in obedience, control, and discipline; and to desire You more than anyone or anything else. Help me always to have a hunger and a thirst and a passion for You.

When temptations arise, I remind myself I am not my own; I have been bought with a price. I have no will but to do His will and no right but to do what is right in His eyes.

If you are in the jaws of temptation, fall on your knees—as many times as it takes—and cry out, "Lord, help me! Deliver me! Protect me! Let Your will prevail!" If you really mean it when you cry out to the Lord, He will provide a way of escape.

Real Satisfaction

For years *Dale* had wanted to have a sexual encounter with *Sandy*. The night he read a preview of this book, he had that encounter—in his dreams. When he started getting what he thought he always wanted, he realized it was not what he really wanted, so he shut it down. The next morning he recalled the dream and felt a great victory was achieved. His perspective on that long desire to have an encounter with *Sandy* changed from an obsession for her to the realization that only the Lord can truly satisfy.

Many people's "highest calling" is to stay in shape and look good for the next sexual exploit. They do not get beyond this until the ravages of age, disease, or an injury take their toll and become irreversible. It is better to stay in shape to faithfully serve the Lord and present your body as a living sacrifice in service to Him.

A married man who had been a womanizer all his life said to me, "I don't understand how you could give up women. You mean to tell me that if the most beautiful woman in the world stood before you and offered you anything, you would refuse it." I responded, "I would, because I have found something better."

He continued, "I can give up anything but women." I responded, "I had every pleasure imaginable, but it did not satisfy me. When you come to have a relationship with the Lord like I do, you will give up anything else that undermines or hinders that relationship because nothing compares to knowing and living for Him."

How fleeting are the things of this world. Knowing the Lord and walking in His presence and victory are more satisfying than pursuing any lust of the flesh.

My relationship with Jesus Christ is more important to me and fulfills and satisfies me more than anyone or anything else—more than sex, pornography, or any other temporary, self-gratifying pleasure this world has to offer. All else is inferior to knowing Him. I never want to lose His presence in my life.

I understand what the psalmist meant when he said, "Besides You, I desire nothing on earth" (Psalm 73:25 NAS), and "As the deer pants for streams of water, so my soul pants for You, O God" (Psalm 42:1).

We serve an amazing God and Creator and can only imagine what He has in store for His faithful servants. One thing is certain, we will be satisfied for all eternity in a universal paradise of His design which contains His manifest presence and blessings beyond the comprehension of mortal minds.

With All Your Strength

When you "love the Lord your God with all your heart and with all your soul and with all your mind and with all your strength" (Mark 12:30), you will limit or remove any influence—television, movies, the Internet, and so on—which takes you away from Him. Instead, you will desire to seek Him through prayer, fasting, and Scripture.

As you do, you will notice a gradual fading of the lusts of the flesh. The temporary pleasures of this world will dim in comparison to knowing Christ. Seeking His will and living a life that honors Him will become your ultimate purpose and desire.

A Storybook Romance

God is faithful and can make storybook romances come to fruition if we trust Him. Although His path is never easy, it is well worth the wait as He accomplishes His purpose. Below are the testimonies of my daughter, Tabitha, and Clayton as they fully commit themselves to the Lord.

Tabitha first met Clayton at a wedding rehearsal. It was during a ministry trip to San Diego in February, 1997, where I performed a wedding ceremony for my nephew Rich and his fiancee, Sunday. Rich's friend, Clayton, a California Highway Patrolman, was a groomsman in the wedding. There at the rehearsal, far from her home in Pennsylvania, Tabitha's and Clayton's eyes met, and the storybook romance began.

When God's Children Pray, He Answers

Little did anyone know at the time that Rich and Sunday, for three years prior to Tabitha's arrival, had been sharing God's Word with Clayton and praying he would totally commit his life to Christ. They had no idea that Tabitha, Rich's cousin, would be the answer to that prayer.

Clayton had been seeking for something more in his life. Although he made a commitment to Christ at the age of twelve and even read the Scriptures, he was unsettled. He was not content with just a form of religiosity.

Upon meeting Tabitha, he suddenly realized what it was. Her vivacious faith and total commitment to the Lord drew him even closer to God. One day out of a deep longing for truth and guidance, he submitted to and recognized Christ as Lord of his life.

A Father's Insight

Three days after Tabitha met Clayton, I saw them talking to one another as they sat on the steps outside our hotel room. I remarked to my wife Karen, "They are going to get married."

Tabitha's Promise—Not As Easy As It Seemed

The year and a half prior to meeting Clayton was like living in a barren wasteland in many respects for Tabitha. It wasn't easy staying home night after night while her friends were dating and having "fun." Tabitha had promised the Lord and herself that she would not date until she found the man who would be her husband. So she spent many long, lonely nights waiting and praying, after turning down many opportunities to date.

Like David of old, Tabitha believed God for the answer to her prayer—

I call on You, O God, for You will answer me; give ear to me and hear my prayer (Psalm 17:6).

Tabitha's Journey West

Even before meeting Clayton, Tabitha and a friend had planned to move to San Diego in search of employment, but those plans fell through. After the wedding of her cousin Rich, Tabitha's desire to journey west for employment was rekindled. She had been seeking a teaching position since graduating from Geneva College, and California now suddenly became a real possibility.

The Lord Works Out the Details

As the Good Book says—

Since You are my rock and my fortress, for the sake of Your name lead and guide me (Psalm 31:3).

And so it was with Tabitha. After seeking employment for over a month while staying at her cousin's apartment in San Diego, the Lord moved. Tabitha was hired at the very school she had desired, and for the teaching position (second grade) she had hoped for. This could not have come at a better time. According to apartment policy, she had stayed close to the end of her allotted time and would soon have to vacate the premises.

Where would she live now that she had a teaching position and had to leave her cousin's apartment? She prayed about it. As she was waiting for God's answer to her prayers and contemplating her possibilities, an apartment opened up unexpectedly right below her cousin's apartment and next door to her future fiance, giving her the perfect living location.

Clayton ended up becoming the husband Tabitha had prayed for so earnestly and waited for so patiently.

Tabitha Writes of Her Love for Clayton

As is my custom with any couple I marry, I asked both Tabitha and Clayton to write in a letter how they met and why they love each other. In answer to my question, "Why do you love Clayton and want to marry him?" Tabitha responded:

> I am going to start from a year and a half before I met him. I remember praying and writing a list of

exactly what I wanted in a husband and thinking, "This list is too unrealistic. I will never find this perfect man." But I was still not going to settle for anything less. I just kept praying. I had decided to quit dating and just let God send him to me.

I spent a year and a half praying and asked God for a couple of things:

1) To have us fall in love with each other's personalities, instead of the superficial way of the world, which focuses on outward appearances.

2) To know when I saw him this was the person I was going to marry. I also kept asking God to send me a man like the one in the list I had written.

My list consisted of—

Appearance: dark hair, blue or green eyes, tall—over 6 feet, good build, athletic, etc.

Personality: the most important thing was he must be a Christian, also able to make me laugh and feel good about myself, love being with others, want to do some type of missions work, and be romantic, and so the list went on and on.

Pretty unrealistic…huh? That's what I thought.

Everything changed on February 13th, a couple of days before my cousin's wedding. I had been hearing from my aunt about Rich's roommate, Clay, who was very good-looking, but not a committed Christian and was really picky and liked to go out and drink, etc. I kept thinking, "Why is everyone telling me about him? This is everything I am trying to stay away from."

I knew I was going to meet him at the wedding, so I was prepared to keep my walls up and let everyone know he was not for me. Well, from the moment I met him, he had my heart. He was nothing like what everyone had said he was!—except for one thing—he was extremely handsome! He had the most beautiful eyes and a smile that made me melt, but of course I would never let him know this.

For three days, we spent much time together. I loved that he loved being around my family. I loved how he was with other people, that he could take charge of a conversation and make people laugh. I loved that he always took time to talk to others. I loved that he was such an awesome conversationalist and an awesome listener, which is an uncommon trait in most men. We spent one night talking for about six hours straight with no one else around, and we never ran out of things to say to one another.

I had a chance to stay for another week and spend more time with Clay and get to know him more. But I prayed about it, and God told me to go home. So Clay and I decided we would see each other again in May.

Most people would think, "Yeah, right. You only spent three days together. You live clear across the country from one another. You are not going to see each other for four months…it will never work."

The night we said good-bye we both had such peace we weren't afraid of what would happen or if we would actually see each other again. We both were filled with a peace that could only come from God, and we both knew this was going to work out. I came home and three days later, I knew this man was the one I was going to marry and spend the rest of my life with. So the phone calls began and the teary nights when I would miss him.

But prayer request number one was answered in that this was a long-distance relationship, and so much of our first couple of months together was spent over the phone talking. I began to realize God answered my prayer of falling in love with one another for our God-given personalities and not just basing it on outward appearance. Talking to one another by phone over the 3,000 miles that separated us caused us to focus on our personalities. As a result, I fell in love with him even more for the wonderful man he really is, and I began to see the real person God had created inside.

I also thought God had answered my second request by sending me my dream man I had written down in a list in my prayer journal. I just could not believe this person I dreamed about was actually a breathing and living being.

Well, let me tell you, dreams do come true. God is so good.

Tabitha, who believed this promise found in God's Word, saw it become a reality in her life—

Delight yourself in the LORD *and He will give you the desires of your heart* (Psalm 37:4).

Clayton Comes to Pennsylvania

When Clayton first visited Tabitha in Pennsylvania in May 1997, I told him as the two of us lifted weights together in the weightlifting room at the ministry center that the three most important things in my life are the Lord, family, and health. I added, "I am entrusting into your care one of the most precious things in the world to me, so do not do anything to violate that trust." He quickly responded, "I love your daughter and will never violate that trust."

Tabitha's faith challenged Clayton to a deeper walk with the Lord. In June he went into the mountains to seek Him with all his heart. It was then that he made a total commitment to Christ and to biblical Christianity.

Clayton Writes of His Love for Tabitha

The following is an e-mail message sent to me from Clayton regarding his love for Tabitha:

> Bill,
> You are asking me why I love your daughter. I can tell you I do love her with all I have…but why? Tabitha had an entire profile set up for the perfect man. I did not have any such tool. What I did use was my heart.
>
> When I met Tabitha, it was as if I had already known her. I felt comfortable with her. We spoke and we spent time together. I knew I could marry her. She was all I ever wanted without ever knowing what that was exactly.
>
> I have never met a woman who had such energy, who was so fun-loving, sincere and grounded in her ways. Her personality in conjunction with her incredible beauty became overpowering. I told Tabitha I was so focused on how comfortable I was around her and how easy it was to get to know her that there was a delay in noticing her eyes and her smile.
>
> Her cousin's wedding was an incredibly romantic time. When she left me to return to Pennsylvania, I had a strange feeling of knowing that I would see her again. I had so much confidence in her word and I believed that she felt the same way. I knew it would be difficult to see her again; she lived across the country. But I just knew it would work. I never worried about it.
>
> We saw each other again and again and we grew closer each time. The next thing I knew, after some time had passed, I confessed to her that I loved her. I was afraid it was too early to tell her because even

if she felt the same way, I could end up scaring her away. It didn't. She sat down with me and confessed the same on an afternoon I will never forget.

As difficult as it is to define love, it is just as difficult to discover the reason for love or how it is created. I do know its origin—God. And I only know that just as God exists so does my love for Tabitha. So, I feel I cannot fully explain why I love Tabitha and at the same time do our love justice…words cannot explain what I feel or why I feel it.

But, let me tell you I believe our love for each other is a gift from God and a direct answer to prayer.

The Proposal

It was the Fourth of July. Clayton was on duty in San Diego and had stopped for his lunch break at the Soup Plantation restaurant where Tabitha, Karen, and other family members were waiting. When we had almost finished eating, Clayton stood up in the restaurant and asked for everyone's attention.

Karen and I thought since Clay was a highway patrolman he was going to warn folks not to drink and drive on the Fourth, or some other public service announcement. Instead, Clay announced to an attentive audience that he loved Tabitha and was asking for her hand in marriage. After he got down on his knee and proposed to her, the people in the restaurant applauded.

God Is Faithful

Four months before the wedding Karen and I began praying and fasting. We needed the Lord's help and blessing. Many of the young adults in the wedding party were from parts of the country where snow was rare and Tabitha had always dreamed of a Christmas wedding with all the accompanying decorations and snow-covered scenery. So Karen and I prayed specifically for snow to blanket the ground for our daughter's special day, yet the roads would be snow free; and for clear weather for those traveling to the ceremony.

Friday, the day Tabitha and Clayton arrived at Cleveland airport, we began to get some snow showers—enough for several members of the bridal party, who were from out west, to engage in nine or ten snowball fights on ministry property during that three-day period.

Sunday, December 7, 1997, as we were about to leave for the church at 2:30 p.m., the snow squalls that were predicted began to fall in earnest, so much so that one of the bridesmaids had to use an umbrella to cover the bride as she went from our van into the church. A short while later the snow had nearly stopped and the sky was clearing.

By 3:00 p.m. the snow had stopped completely, the roads were snow free, and the sky had cleared. This enabled many of the folks who cannot go out in slippery weather to attend the ceremony and travel afterwards to the reception several miles away. The large church sanctuary was packed for the ceremony and many commented that it was the most beautiful wedding they had ever attended.

On Monday, as family and friends and the bride and groom were going back to the airport at Cleveland, half the snow was already melting or gone and there was no new snow for several weeks. We are convinced that having snow on the ground, yet snow-free roads, was a wedding gift from the Lord and another confirmation.

During the wedding ceremony I stated:

> Tabitha, from the time you were in your
> mother's womb we prayed for you and dedicated
> you to the Lord. We raised you to fear and honor the
> Lord. You have been the best daughter any parents

could ask. We prayed and fasted you would one day marry the mate of God's choice. We believe you are doing so. In love we commit you to the Lord and to Clayton to take care of you physically, emotionally, and spiritually.

Was This All Merely Coincidence?

Tabitha lived in Hermitage, Pennsylvania and Clayton lived 3,000 miles away in San Diego, California. What were the chances of the two of them meeting? What were the chances of Tabitha finding a teaching job seemingly out of nowhere in a Christian school and in the grade she desired to teach? What were the odds for that "unexpected" vacancy in the apartment complex to open up? What were the odds that Tabitha would find a husband to match her list of criteria?

Was it mere coincidence there was snow in place for the wedding with cleared streets when two weeks before and two weeks after there was no snow? Or is it that indeed there is an infinite, personal God, who cares about the details of our lives? Surely all of these events that have transpired in only a year's time can only be attributed to the workings of a gracious God and a heavenly Father who honors His covenant with His children who love and honor Him.

Many more amazing events have since then occurred in the lives of Tabitha and Clayton.

A Modern-Day Love Story

You just read Tabitha and Clayton's storybook romance in the previous chapter. A couple of years later my son, BJ, and Tara got married. Now here is their modern day love story which is another confirmation that sexuality when properly understood can be a very beautiful and romantic experience—the way God intended it to be.

Like his sister Tabitha, BJ was dedicated to the Lord while in his mother's womb. My wife and I prayed and fasted that both our daughter and our son would marry the person of God's choice and fulfill the calling and purpose the Lord had on their lives and families. So how did the Lord do it?

BJ was a senior in high school and Tara was a freshman when they met at a basketball game. After months of glances and flirting in the halls, BJ asked Tara out on a date. She knew her father would never allow her to date, so after she and her mother worked on him, on February 17, 1994, BJ and Tara had their first date.

BJ's Story

BJ relates the following:

> The first time I saw Tara was at a Hickory High School basketball game. I remember thinking, "Wow,

she is so pretty!" For the next year, I saw her at more basketball games, Buhl Park dances, and in the hallway at school. During this time, our relationship consisted merely of eye glancing and an occasional hello.

Finally, I got tired of the casual flirting and I decided to ask her out on a date. I cannot lie, the main reason I asked her out was because she was so beautiful. However, after a few dates I realized that her beauty was not only external but also internal.

I can visualize in my head the exact details of how I asked her out. She was walking to math class, so as I walked by her I romantically said, "Hey, you wanna go out some time?" She told me later she thought I was joking so she did not respond. Several days later, instead of just walking by, I stopped at her locker. This time she said "yes" and the following day, we had our first date.

There is no greater joy than when you finally find the person God wants you to marry. I can remember the day I knew, without doubt, God wanted me to marry Tara. We had been going through difficulties in our relationship. As a result, we decided to take a month away from each other, and after this time see if we wanted to get back together. While we were apart, I spent a lot of time in prayer trying to figure out what I should do. I knew that if we got back together it was with the intention to get married.

At the conclusion of the month, Tara and I decided to meet at Buhl Park and share what God had laid on our hearts in regard to our relationship. I was so nervous to see her. I had no idea what to say to her because I was still unsure of what God wanted.

Before we met, I asked God to somehow give me a sign as to whether or not she was the one that He wanted me to marry. Sure enough, God answered my prayer. There was a rainbow over Lake Julia. The moment I saw Tara's face I knew that I would marry her. As tears of joy rolled down my face, Tara and I agreed before the Lord that we wanted to spend the rest of our lives together. From that day on, I knew Tara was going to be my wife.

My roommate and I were talking about relationships and marriages. We were discussing various attributes and qualities that one should look for in a girl. After talking for a while, I said the following to him. "If the girl you are dating brings you closer to Jesus Christ then you know you have a special person, but if she draws you away from Him, then you better run from her and not look back."

God has used Tara in my life to draw me closer to Him. All the degrees that I possess do not equal what I have learned from her. I thank God everyday for her because she has a passion and love for the same One that I do—Jesus Christ.

It is an honor and a privilege when you get the chance to marry your best friend; when you get to spend the rest of your life with the person who knows your hidden dreams and passions; and when this person is the one who stands behind you and encourages you and sacrifices all they have to support you in what God has called you to do.

I thank God every day that I have Tara as my best friend. Everything that I have been able to accomplish in the past is only because she has been there cheering me on. She is my greatest fan and I am privileged to call her my wife.

I wrote the following to my father before he married us:

Why do I want to marry Tara? The main reason is not because she fills some void in my life, nor is it because life only has meaning with her as my wife. I want to marry Tara because I yearn every day to show her how much I love her. I want to wake up every morning and go to bed every night telling her the three most precious words I can say, "I love you." I look forward to seeing her smile; I love to watch her face glow with happiness. Tara is God's blessing to me. Just as He has loved me, He has given her to me to show the same selfless love: A love that is willing to sacrifice all to serve her. My promise to Tara before God is that in all my strength and in all my weakness I will love her for the rest of my life. As Jesus gave His life for the world, I give my life to her.

Tara's Story

Tara relates the following:

I remember meeting BJ at a basketball game. His friends were very nice. I would see BJ a lot, but we didn't talk much at first. I remember thinking he was cute, but he was always flirting with girls and I even saw him kiss a girl, so I never bothered with him.

When I was in third grade I remember admiring my grandma. I wanted to be more like her. What I admired was her love for God. I remember praying and asking Jesus to be with me and help me be a better person. Little did I know the little Catholic girl had just said her own sinner's prayer.

All through my years at CCD (Confraternity of Christian Doctrine), I didn't learn much. But I remember the day we got to read from the Bible and how I loved it. My other grandma and great-grandma always had Bibles and I would read theirs but I didn't understand much.

The point of telling you this is to show you that I was searching. I just wasn't sure what for.

I remember in eighth grade saying a prayer. I asked God to show me the person I would marry. I did not want to date a million guys. I wanted to be like my parents and find that one person I was supposed to be with forever.

I actually forgot about that prayer for a while. Then at the Buhl Park dance BJ came over and put his arm around me. I melted inside, but he asked me to dance with his friend. I was disappointed. Then I saw BJ with some girl and I was totally upset. I thought he was such a jerk the way he acted with all the girls. I was determined to keep my distance from this guy.

In the fall of 1993, I saw this blonde guy giving a speech for the soccer team at "Meet the Team" night. My friend said, look how gorgeous he is. I melted inside again. Wow!

He was hot! I said, "Who is he?" And she said, "You know who…BJ Rudge!"

The school year went on. I would see him at school and he would still be flirting with girls. I would smile and walk away. I never approached him. I think this is what made him curious about me. I was the one girl that didn't throw herself at him. Part of it was because I figured he wouldn't want me, part of it was because I thought he was a jerk for being such a flirt, and part was because I wasn't allowed to date yet.

Somehow, I was in the only freshman homeroom in the senior hallway right beside BJ's room.

Gradually our chats became more frequent. I can admit first liking him at the Christmas chorus concert. He fixed his hair different and he looked like such a nerd! But for some reason I was starting to have a crush by laughing at him. I remember telling my mom that I liked him and she encouraged it because his dad was a minister. "He must be a nice kid," she said.

Anyway, we soon were flirting at school events and in the halls between classes. I knew he liked me, but I wasn't allowed to date so I figured there was no point. I think this helped me not to be an easy catch.

He asked me out once and I just stood there. I didn't answer because I thought he was either kidding or trying to make fun of me. Besides, I wasn't allowed to date. What is a girl to do? Nothing. Almost ten days went by and I was getting books out of my locker when these soccer shoes stepped beside me. I looked up and it was him. After I slowed my heart down, I tried to control my blushing and my throat jumping out of me. I stood up and smiled. He asked me out and I said "yes" this time.

After my mom and I worked on my dad to let me go out, we went to see the movie "My Girl Two" and to eat TCBY yogurt.

We had decided not to get serious because he would be leaving for college and I was so young, but as you know that didn't work. I remember BJ saying to me, "I 'loke' you," but he was scared to admit he was falling in love. "I'm growing fond of you," he said. The first time he said, "I love you" was when I stayed home from a basketball game with him because he was sick. And he wrote it in my hand with his finger. "I love U!"

BJ went to Geneva College and came home on weekends. I remember getting in a fight before he left and he told me I was the first girl he thought he could marry. At this point, I knew that I loved him too!

Of course, you know we had many issues to work out with religion and Christianity. It wasn't easy because I always did have a personal relationship with Jesus and was Catholic. What I didn't have was a commitment.

Soon, my relationship with God bloomed and so did our relationship. We had many hard times and fights. Just when we came to the breaking point and thought we could never make it through anymore, we prayed and prayed. I remember asking God for a sign to show me what was right. We went for a walk in the park and saw a rainbow. And BJ said, "Do you think it's a sign?" I knew it was.

We had a long haul ahead of us. I wasn't even sure that I wanted to be with him or could forgive him for everything. It was hard.

Then one day he took me out for ice cream and bought me a rose. He read a letter to me telling me how much he loved me and how sorry he was. He started to cry. I asked him why and he said because, "I just realized I am sitting across from the person I am going to spend the rest of my life with." It was at that moment I knew he was the one for me.

I want to marry BJ because I love him. After all the break-ups and fights, we could never stay apart from each other. No one can make me madder or happier than BJ. No matter how hurt or upset I am, when he hugs me, I am okay and I feel safe and I feel peace.

I love the fact he reminds me of my dad in so many ways that others can't even see. I love the fact he shows me how to love. He showed me the love of Jesus Christ. And he makes me a better person. I love the fact no matter how mad I am, when he smiles, even my stubborn self has to give in. I love the way he listens to me whine and complain. He waits till I stress out completely and then tells me to calm down.

I love the fact we don't let each other give up. We both give "tough love" when we need it. When I am weak, he is strong and when he is weak, I am strong. We complete each other. He says he wants to have more "child-like faith" and I want to have more biblical knowledge. I love the fact I know he is always there for me no matter what time of day—even 3,000 miles apart.

I want to marry him because he is my best friend. I hate saying good-bye at night. I want to wake up and know that he is beside me. I am anxious to see what God has for our lives together. Where we will go? What we will do? How many kids we will have and what they will look like?

All I know is that I love BJ and I want to spend the rest of my life with him and trust God together to meet our needs.

The Proposal

BJ's comments about the proposal:

It was five years after our first date that I proposed to Tara. We had been discussing marriage a month prior and had looked at different engagement rings. Finally, I found just the right one I wanted to give Tara.

I began to plan this romantic day for us. However, these plans quickly changed. The day I got the ring, I had to give it to her. I was leaving in a month for California to get my master's degree. I had plans of proposing in a hot air balloon or over a loud speaker on the plane on my way to California, but when I got the ring, I couldn't wait.

It was November 18, 1998. I do not know exactly why, but I just had to give her the ring. In the small amount of time I had, I planned how I would propose. At that time, Tara was a hostess at Hickory Grille. I called her manager on the phone and told her that I was planning on coming in after Tara got off work and propose to her.

As Tara's shift came to an end I showed up and told her I wanted to get dessert. Having a taste for sweets Tara had no objection. After eating our dessert, I arranged for one of my friends to bring in a box of roses. He brought them in to the delight of Tara. She had no idea that there was an engagement ring inside.

As her eyes got big and tears rolled down her face, I got the attention of the entire restaurant. Getting down on one knee I said to her, "I want to spend the rest of my life with you, will you marry me?" She responded by saying, "Yes."

After being engaged only one month, I left for California. This separation lasted a year and a half, and believe me it was not easy. I missed seeing Tara's smiling face. But I am thankful that I was at least able to hear her voice over the phone. This time away proved to be a challenge for our relationship, but through it, God brought us even closer.

God Fulfills His Plan

BJ and Tara were apart six years while BJ went to college and then for his master's degree and Tara went to nursing school. During their two-year engagement they only saw each other every couple of months. They knew how hard it was to maintain purity while dating for so many years, but this strengthened their commitment to their relationship while dating and later helped build trust in their marriage. They knew they could trust each other not to ever cheat.

BJ and Tara are now married and they both will tell you that it was worth the wait to remain virgins until marriage. BJ completed his doctorate degree after marrying Tara and is now serving in full-time ministry.

Closing Comments

Storybook romances can happen if we are willing to be faithful to God as we await His timing for us. Praying for the right mate and remaining pure will definitely eventually prove to be an asset. However, not all people are expected to marry and God will bless singles as well as married couples.

It does not matter what your circumstances or life situation might be, God has a plan and a purpose for you. It does not matter whether you are married to the love of your life, or feel trapped in a marriage or an unmarried state that you feel powerless to change.

When we choose to honor the Lord with our lives, He takes whatever we have to offer, including our circumstances, and begins to work them together for good and to accomplish His purpose.

Your circumstances may not necessarily change as past choices sometimes last a lifetime—but He will change you. And He will give you the wisdom and fortitude necessary to change what you can and to be content in what you cannot change.

He Will Be Faithful

Overcoming sexual immorality can seem daunting. However, God will give you the strength you need to tear down the strongholds and to be all that He intended you to be—even in our sex-crazed culture.

He will be faithful to help you not only to persevere but to overcome and triumph, like the victor in a great contest. His path is never an easy one, but it is always the most rewarding—both in this life and the one to come.

FOR MORE INFORMATION

Bill Rudge has produced numerous books, pamphlets, and CDs on a variety of timely topics. For a complete listing or a copy of his informative newsletter, visit our web site or write to:

Bill Rudge Ministries
P.O. Box 108
Sharon, PA 16146
U.S.A.

www.billrudge.org

 JT Kalnay is an attorney and an author. He has been an athlete, a soldier, a professor, a programmer, an Ironman, and mountain climber. JT now divides his time between being an attorney, being an author, and helping his wife chase after seven nieces and nephews.

JT was born and raised in Belleville, Ontario, Canada. Growing up literally steps from the Bay of Quinte, water, ice, fishing, swimming, boating, and drowning were very early influences and appear frequently in his work.

Educated at the Royal Military College, the University of Ottawa, the University of Dayton, and Case Western Reserve University, JT has spent countless hours studying a wide range of subjects including math, English, computer science, and law. Many of his stories are set on college campuses.

JT is a certified rock climbing guide and can often be found atop crags in West Virginia, California, Mexico, and Italy. Rock climbing appears frequently in his writing.

JT has witnessed firsthand many traumatic events including the World Trade Center Bombing, the Long Island Railroad Shooting, a bear attack, a plane crash, and numerous fatalities, in the mountains and elsewhere.

Connect with jt online at:
www.jtkalnay.com
http://jtkalnaynovels.wordpress.com